\-

The Shidduch Crisis

Causes and Cures

THE SHIDDUCH CRISIS

CAUSES AND CURES

MICHAEL J. SALAMON

URIM PUBLICATIONS
Jerusalem • New York

The Shidduch Crisis
by Michael J. Salamon

Layout design by Satya Levine
Printed at Hemed Press, Israel. First Edition.
ISBN 13: 978-965-524-006-1
ISBN 10: 965-524-006-1

Urim Publications
P.O. Box 52287, Jerusalem 91521 Israel

Lambda Publishers Inc.
3709 13th Avenue Brooklyn, New York 11218 U.S.A.
Tel: 718-972-5449 Fax: 718-972-6307, mh@ejudaica.com

www.UrimPublications.com

⬛⬛⬛ CONTENTS ⬛⬛⬛

INTRODUCTION

As a PSYCHOLOGIST, I am often asked serious and important questions about the individuals I work with. However, since I am bound by the laws of confidentiality, without a properly executed release form from the person I treated, I do not even acknowledge the names of individuals I may have worked with. This does not deter some self-appointed detectives from calling and asking repeatedly, particularly when it comes to trying to get information that some feel is relevant to a shidduch that they may be exploring. Witness this recent phone call:

> CALLER: Dr. Salamon, I am calling because I have to find out some important information regarding a shidduch.

> DR. S.: Of course, you know that I am not at liberty to discuss any private information. Not only is it illegal; it is unethical.

> CALLER: This situation is different.

> DR. S.: I am afraid that there is no situation that is different unless the people involved give explicit permission.

CALLER: Well, they don't know that I am calling, but they have spoken highly of you and I was asked to get this information so that we can decide to proceed with the shidduch or not.

DR. S.: I still cannot give you such information.

CALLER: Well, let me ask the question anyway and you will see how important it is for the decision-making process. So the question is: At what age was this young man toilet-trained?

I did not answer the question and was perhaps even rude because I simply hung up at that point. That did not dissuade the caller from trying to reach me at my office two more times and once more at my home. The question, which may have some relevance to understanding early childhood development or the development of a psycho-educational intervention for a young child, was extremely inappropriate in this or almost any other context. I was upset by the question and the tenacity of the caller in trying to convince me of its relevance. I had fielded questions in the past regarding possible mental illness in the family of a prospective date as well as a family's history of physical ailments. Questions ranged from whether there was a family member who suffered from diabetes, cancer or multiple sclerosis and at what age the disease was contracted or diagnosed. I never reveal information and I am of the opinion that, except for genetic diseases, which will be discussed later, questions regarding illness are almost always irrelevant because there is no likelihood that any family will be without a history of some illness. However, the question about toilet training got me to thinking in even greater depth about what has gone wrong in the shidduch scene.

The questions now asked by shadchanim (matchmakers) and family members have evolved from the foolish and superficial "color of the tablecloth" ones to questions that appear important but are often merely destructive and represent *lashon ha-ra* (gossip, literally "evil talk"). Young men and women make lists of what they want in a mate, which is often little more than an exercise in fantasy. Throughout this text we will look at some of the newer types of questions included in these lists and try to evaluate their origin, evolution and goals.

The difficulty of the questions relates to the difficulty of the entire shidduch process and does not appear to address the real issues of what attracts people and helps to keep them together. Parents struggle to find the right match for their child while their children struggle to find their identities within the context of an increasingly divided and thus divisive community. The pressure on all sides is intense and getting worse. When family members and friends try to help, the result is often even more conflict and pain.

When I began dating, the only questions my parents asked were: "What neighborhood does she live in, and what shul does the family daven in?" Things have changed dramatically since then. We recently had an experience in our own family in which a friend tried to assist a family member with a date. The friend, who knows both the young man in our family, who was twenty-four at the time, and the young woman being recommended, called the young man to suggest the contact. "In fact," she said, "I have her cellphone number so that you can call her directly and not go through any additional parties." The young man consented, took the phone number and called the very next day. However, the one who answered was not the young woman but her father, who proceeded to question him for the next thirty minutes. The grilling included some standard though not completely relevant or anticipated questions such as long-term life plans and goals, where he went to school and how much he is learning at present. The young man took the questioning in relatively good humor and responded well. When the father completed his questioning he said to the young man, "You can speak with my daughter now." The young man answered, "No, thank you," and hung up.

Most people who have heard this story asked why the young man did not hang up on the woman's father immediately. Some derided him for not speaking with the girl after her father gave his permission. His response was that while he respected the father's right to ask questions and advocate for his daughter, it was clear that the father did not allow his twenty-three-year-old daughter to be an adult capable of finding out important information for herself.

For many years now I, together with many colleagues, have witnessed an increase in marital problems that are often related to a profound lack of readiness for marriage and children, unrealistic expectations about marriage, or even a simple lack of understanding of the individual's own personality. Part of this is due to a general overprotectiveness on the part of parents these days. Since parents want to make sure that their children are well taken care of, they continue to make decisions for them, not allowing them to grow up, mature and develop a sense of self. This is clear in the story of the father taking the call for his adult daughter and interrogating the caller.

The other component is an almost narcissistic denial of one's own shortcomings and seeing weakness only in others. Why else would someone want to know at what age someone was toilet-trained? Would the fact that a child was trained at twenty-four or thirty months say anything at all about whether or not a couple can form a strong marriage? How would this information be useful in preparing the couple for marriage? Of course, one can rationalize that bedwetting may be genetic, but how would that make for a stronger or weaker marriage? The final component seems to be related to a universal move toward greater rigidity.

We have begun to believe that the more strict, demanding and unyielding we become, the better our lives will be. Yet this rigidity has not enhanced our lives. Perhaps it is time to reevaluate our goals and bring some intellectual honesty and common sense back to the dating process. This in no way negates the need for a shadchan when one is required or in those groups where a shadchan is part of the process. Yet neither does it negate the need for other healthy means of finding the right mate. It is time that we cease to confuse tradition, personal bias or even obsessions with honest, reasonable and Halachic approaches to dating and finding the right mate.

ACKNOWLEDGEMENTS

THE IDEA FOR THIS BOOK originally grew out of a series of lectures and talks that I gave. I am grateful for the opportunity that those speaking engagements afforded me to interact with many different people, hear their ideas and help me to formulate and articulate my own ideas more clearly.

Several people and groups were instrumental in helping this text come to fruition. My staff, particularly Indra, was supportive and encouraging and acted as cheerleaders for the completion of this project. My extended family, who while sitting around a celebratory dinner table pushed me to finish the book and have it published, deserves tremendous thanks, which I humbly offer them. Together with Naomi, my wife, our children, Avi, Keren, Moshe, Bryan and Deborah, insisted that the book is important and should see the light of day.

To the hundreds of people who offered their experiences, not simply clinically but with personal vignettes, I offer my sincerest gratitude. It was as if people who had heard of this project and wanted to share what happened to them suddenly thrust a tidal wave of their experiences upon me. Particularly noteworthy in this group are Pam, Max, Charles, Pearl, Jerry, Steven, Bracha, Uri and Shmuel, all of whom are strong believers in Am Yisroel and who work tirelessly to alleviate its difficulties.

My agent, Candace Plotsker-Herman of Creative Communication, also pushed me to finish this book and kept at me until I did. Experience is a strong motivator, and the many rabbis who told me that they would welcome my text did so with their profound knowledge and experience with the problem. The statement I most often heard, "Something has to be done," became a rallying point.

I also would like to thank the people who told me to be wary of publishing this book. Their kind warnings that it might affect my wife, our children and me were meant to be protective, but instead were motivating.

Perhaps my biggest motivator to publish this book was and remains the desire to help people avoid the pitfalls that I often see in my clinical practice and to enhance the mitzvah of *ve-ahavta le-re'acha kamocha*.

CHAPTER 1

HAVE WE LOST OUR COMMON SENSE?

SHADCHAN TO MOTHER OF A YOUNG WOMAN: "Does she wear a seat belt in the car?"

MOTHER: "Of course."

SHADCHAN: "Well, that could be a problem with this particular family."

■ ■ ■ ■ ■

SHADCHAN TO A YOUNG MAN: "Do you wear lace or slip-on shoes? Does your Shabbos hat have a feather in it?"

■ ■ ■ ■ ■

Rivka heard that her friend Toby was going to a wedding out of town. She knew that Toby would be taking the bus that the family had provided for the guests, as would a young man named Avi. Since Rivka had some passing interest in Avi, she asked Toby to speak with him, find out more about him and see whether or not she should be introduced to him. Toby agreed and spent several hours talking with Avi on the bus ride to and from the wedding. During the conversation it became clear to both Toby and Avi that they had a great deal in common and that they were interested in spending more time together. Unfortunately, neither of them knew anyone who could introduce them officially. Their relationship languished for months until finally one got up the nerve to call the other. Now that they have been happily married for several years, they are hoping to find a way to make the introduction and dating process easier for other couples.

■ ■ ■ ■ ■

On her way to her cousin's wedding in Florida, my daughter found herself sitting next to a nice, frum young man on a JetBlue flight. He asked her where she was going and a conversation ensued. It turned out that he was going to the same wedding and was a close friend of the groom, who was her cousin. They spent the flight talking and began dating several weeks later. Several months later, they were engaged.

Two weeks before the wedding, I received a phone call from someone asking me, "How can you let this happen?" I was not sure what he was referring to. Was there perhaps some significant problem that had been hidden from the couple or their parents that should delay the wedding? When I asked him what it might be, he answered that there was no problem with the boy or his family. The problem was simply that "This is not the way things are done!" I cynically thanked him for his wishes, and just before I hung up, I asked him how he met his wife and how his parents had met. I knew perfectly well that regardless of his family's particular hashkafa, the odds were excellent that he and his wife had met at a social function, as had his parents.

I have reviewed several books on dating that are available to young people. While some have reasonably good suggestions and funny stories, most are rather sad. For example, almost every book suggests that the young man brush his hat and polish his shoes before going on a date. Setting aside the issue of whether a hat is mandatory for a date, shouldn't grooming skills be mastered before the age of ten? Also, if a young man is ready to date seriously and wants to get married, yet he does not know how to make sure that he appears presentable, doesn't that strongly suggest that he is not ready?

The question of the girl wearing a seatbelt is also disturbing. Safety is a priority. We try to teach our children to stay healthy and protect themselves. We do not want them to smoke because of the danger to their health. When they are young, we train them not to run out into the street. When we put them in a car, we tell them to fasten their seatbelts. In some Hasidic families, men drive and women sit in the back seat. Still, they wear seatbelts.

When the shadchan asked the question about the girl wearing the seatbelt, she was serious. The young man and woman did not date. It seems that the young man's family felt that if the young woman wore a seatbelt, the chest strap would heighten her physical attraction, causing the young man to lose control of himself. Of course, it would not be the young man's fault but rather the fault of the young woman, who was behaving immodestly by wearing a seat belt.

I recently met with the father of a young woman who was dating a young man from a wonderful family. His rosh yeshiva has nothing but praise for this young man who, in addition to being a strong learner, is planning to attend medical school while continuing to learn. The couple dated for close to four months and it seemed that there would soon be a marriage proposal.

Unfortunately, when the girl's mother caught the young man chewing gum, she demanded that the relationship be ended. The father thought his wife's decision was hasty and "a terrible mistake." Since he believed that his daughter and her gum-chewing young man would make a wonderful couple, he asked me to speak with his wife. However, the rosh yeshiva had already spoken with her. She was adamant that she was right in making her daughter break off the relationship because chewing gum *"passt nisht."* Out of curiosity I asked the mother if the young man smoked. I was told that the question was irrelevant because since many young men in yeshiva smoke, smoking would not disqualify him. In this case smoking, which can cause serious illness and death, was more acceptable than occasional gum-chewing!

I had a similar occurrence with a young man who wore khaki trousers when he picked up his date. In this situation, the father forbade further dates even though he had previously approved of the young man. The couple had gone out at least five times and they had gone bowling on that particular date, an activity that called for khaki pants. Yet here too, it was a case of *passt nisht.*

These few examples indicate a reliance on *lashon ha-ra* and an appalling lack of common sense. Although *lashon ha-ra* is prohibited, the shidduch process seems to be dependent upon it.[1] These days the task of the shadchan, whether a professional matchmaker or a family friend, seems to be to gather as much information as possible, no matter how irrelevant or even untrue it may be. If this information damages or destroys a person's reputation, so be it.

---

[1] Winston, Hella. *Unchosen: The Hidden Lives of Hasidic Rebels.* Boston, MA: 2005.

As I noted above, many of the questions asked do little to illuminate the individual's true character. Frequently they are little more than "a medium in which slander and gossip are nurtured."[2] To be fair, it is necessary to find out information about the young people who will be dating. But the types of questions asked and the way the information is presented hardly provide the necessary insight and actually divert attention from important issues that should be addressed.

The Chofetz Chaim, in his work *Shemirat ha-Lashon* (Mekor ha-Hayyim, Tziun 3), discusses what is considered appropriate to ask people and how one should answer when asked about individuals who are dating. He cites an example of comparing someone to his age-mates and how, by way of this comparison, this individual can be made to seem like a simpleton. He refers to this as *motzi shem ra* (giving someone a bad name), which is clearly not allowed. The Chofetz Chaim specifically states that it is forbidden to defame someone because of something that his father did. One may ask about specific illnesses that the individual may have, a clear lack of morality or *apikorsus* (lack of belief in God). But one may not ask about limited learning abilities or any other questions that affect the relationship because such comparisons are not productive and constitute *lashon ha-ra*. In fact, in the 1950s the Chazon Ish stated that the most important question regarding the young man is often omitted. "Did you ask if he would make a good husband? If that is lacking, it is not a good match regardless of his other qualities."[3]

In our day, people often disregard the Chofetz Chaim's guidelines in an effort to ascertain information that is ultimately of limited value. Later

---

[2] Lamm, Dr. J. "Shidduchim: Is this the way it should be?" *The Jewish Press,* November 8, 2002.

[3] Lorincz, S. *Be-mehitzatam shel gedolei ha-torah,* vol. 1. Jerusalem: 2006, 106.

in this book, we will look at standard shadchan questionnaires and recommended approaches.

THE CRISES

The difficulty with dating is not unique to the Jewish community. In the general population, women are delaying the dating process in favor of starting their careers. While this is not necessarily a crisis, men like the idea of avoiding commitment, which then puts pressure on women who are ready for one. While some of these issues have seeped into the Jewish world, other issues unique to our society exacerbate the situation for our dating children and for ourselves, their parents.

Unfortunately, it is clear that several crises in our community are related in one way or another to the current shidduch approach. These range from a shortage of men to increasing rates of divorce, domestic violence, eating disorders, greater use of medication and, ultimately, leaving the fold entirely.

A detailed article in a recent issue of the *Jerusalem Post* [4] explored reasons why "there is a burgeoning surplus of eligible Jewish females looking to marry, and a major shortfall in available Jewish men." The article indicated that birth rates are not the cause for this three-to-one, female-to-male disparity in the Jewish community. Rather, the reasons tend to be related to the dating process itself.

---

[4] Weiss, S. "Why the guy gap?" *The Jerusalem Post,* December 20, 2005 (available online). Also see http://www.thejewishweek.com/news/newscontent.php3?artid=9308. One may find additional material at www.jewishpress.com by doing a search on its site for "shidduch crisis."

For example, men date a wider range of women and, as a result, tend to marry out of the community more often than women do. Since men are not as likely as women to crave a committed relationship, they are more content to take their time than women are before they settle down in a marriage. With the divorce rate estimated to be as high as thirty percent, men are more likely to say that they do not want to make a mistake.

Within the frum community in particular, Jewish educators report that women are more likely to maintain or increase their religious involvement, while men are more likely to drop out of religious practice even if they maintain the externals.

Essentially, the author of the *Jerusalem Post* article found that marriage is a "buyer's market" exclusively for men. As a result, the men and their representatives ask "any question that comes to mind" – from a prospective date's salary to her dress size or even her mother's. Many families hide disabled children, and some parents "offer men large sums of money to marry their daughters." *Lashon ha-ra,* which has become a mainstay of the dating process, contributes to this aspect of the crisis.

■ ■ ■ ■ ■

Another significant indicator of the crisis in the shidduch scene is the increasing divorce rate. It is important to note that the actual divorce rate in the United States for the general population never exceeded 40 percent and is currently at approximately 30 percent. Actual rates of divorce in the frum community are difficult to find and track in the United States. Perhaps no one wants to really know just how bad it is. Yet anecdotal data indicates that the rates of divorce are rapidly increasing, particularly among young married couples. A review of divorce rates in the New York metropolitan area (see the JOFA web page at www.jofa.org)

indicates that the six major *batei din* (rabbinical courts) perform approximately one thousand divorces per year. These include the Bet Din of Elizabeth, New Jersey, the Bet Din of Agudat Harabonim, the Bet Din of Agudat Harabonim of Brooklyn, the Bet Din of America, the Bet Din L'Inyanei Agunot and the Bais Din of Igud Harabonim of America. There are many other smaller rabbinical courts that do not provide information on rates. To the best of our knowledge, few of these organizations keep statistics about the age of those divorcing or how many years they have been married.

There is also some particularly relevant information from Israel. One very good source of information is a publication of the Israel Central Bureau of Statistics entitled *Vital Statistics: Marriages and Divorces 1999.*[5] This report is extensive and contains information that is both analyzed historically and is as current as 1999. The study also breaks down information by religion and religious beliefs. What is most relevant from the report is that the rate of marriages among Jews has been steadily declining from 9.3 marriages per thousand in the 1970s to 6.6 per thousand in the 1990s, while the divorce rate has been steadily rising. In fact, the divorce rate has doubled in the same period of time, and is highest among those under twenty-five.

A recent report in the Israeli newspaper *Yediot Aharonot*[6] entitled "Tel Aviv: Israel's Divorce Capital" reported some more recent trends. Although the divorce rate for 2005 dropped about two percent, it still hovers around thirty percent for the country as a whole. In Jerusalem, the divorce rate rose by two percent, and some Haredi communities reported

---

[5] Available at www.cbs.gov.il/publications/vital99/vi1198-e.pdf/.

[6] Available at http://www.ynetnews.com/articles/0,7340,L-3200981,00.html/.

a significant increase in the divorce rate. For example, the divorce rate in the town of Betar Illit practically doubled from 2004 to 2005.

As noted, information about divorce rates in the frum communities in the United States is not as easy to come by. Although the number of divorces handled by the Beit Din of America has been steadily increasing, there is no information readily available about variables such as number of years the couple was married, how they met or the number of their children at the time of the divorce.

An attempt to find some current useful data revealed a web site that employed a novel method for exploring divorce trends in the frum community. Using information that is available on the dating site Frumster.com, the author compiled information over a period of two years, 2004 and 2005.[7] There are quite a few problems with this type of research, particularly the fact that those who post on the Frumster.com site are self-selected, the information that they post may not be completely accurate and the number of people available for study is relatively small. Still there is something to be said for the information, which yielded the following results: women under thirty years of age who advertised for a date and considered themselves either modern orthodox *machmir* or yeshivish have higher divorce rates and are more likely to be single parents than others who posted on Frumster.com. While these labels may seem arbitrary and divisive, they provide some framework for understanding some trends. We will have more to say about the labels later on.

Fifty nine percent of those under twenty-five who are divorced have at least one child – a truly disturbing statistic. The author of the study concluded that while the information available for analysis has its

---

[7] www.yutopia.com: see Frumstats 2005.

shortcomings, it appeared that the social pressure to marry young and the lack of maturity to deal properly with the responsibilities of married life feed this increasing trend.

> Riva felt a strong attraction to Dan, who was determined, strong-willed and very handsome. When Dan proposed to Riva after their sixth date, she accepted. It was not long thereafter that Riva began to see an aggressive side to Dan. They were driving together after a party three weeks before their own wedding when a car cut them off. Dan started screaming and took off after the other car. He cut that driver off, slammed on his brakes, jumped out of his car and ran to the other car, where he proceeded to bang on the window and kick the car.

> Riva went home and told her parents, who were very concerned and called the shadchan. The shadchan assured them that she had not heard anything about Dan's temper and the wedding took place as planned. In retrospect, Riva says that she should have broken up with Dan at that point, since soon after the birth of their first child, Dan's behavior changed dramatically. He became verbally abusive and often did not come home until four or five in the morning. Soon after that, he began to hit her. Riva was too afraid to tell anyone.

> One night after their second child was born, Dan came home and beat Riva with a telephone. Neighbors heard Riva crying and called the police. The district attorney had the court issue an order of protection against Dan.

> Dan and Riva had been married for four years and are now in the process of getting a divorce. Riva has two concerns: that she receive custody of the children and that she not be left as an agunah.

Psychologists are often called upon to deal with domestic violence or abuse that occurs within families. This form of abuse within the family unit can be physical, emotional or sexual, and it occurs in all types of relationships in all ethnic and religious groups. The rate of domestic abuse is generally between twenty-five and thirty-five percent,[8] and does not appear to be any different within the Jewish community.[9]

Over the past five years I have noticed an increase in the reporting of domestic violence in my practice, particularly among women who were married for less than ten years. In an attempt to determine whether this was unique to me or something that colleagues were discovering as well, I surveyed other mental health professionals, who reported a similar increase. Here, as in divorce rates, specific numbers are not available, but many anecdotes combine to indicate a trend. Several colleagues reported that they were involved in situations where a shadchan had failed to disclose allegations of a potential partner's history of abusive behavior. Sometimes, as reported in the *Florida Jewish News* by Avi Frier (January 19, 2007), the information is just too deeply hidden from the public, while at other times the shadchan was aware of the allegations but refused to believe them. The result is that an introduction is made, the couple marries and an innocent person becomes a victim of abuse. In some cases

---

[8] Plichta, S.B., and Falik, M. "The Prevalence of Violence and Its Implications for Women's Health." *Women's Health Issues* 11 (2001): 244–258.

[9] Jewish Women International. *A Portrait of Domestic Abuse in the Jewish Community.* Washington, DC: May, 2004. (Cf. www.womanabuseprevention.com.)

the shadchan defended their act of non-disclosure by blaming the partner, saying, "It is the partner's responsibility to see if they are compatible."

There is domestic violence in the Jewish community, and only recently have there been some noteworthy reviews of the problems.[10] Key findings from the Jewish Women International (JWI) Portrait of Domestic Abuse study indicate the following:

1. Domestic abuse in the Jewish community has no boundaries; it affects all types of relationships, all socio-economic classes, all ages and all spectrums of religious and cultural life… including sexual, verbal, psychological, physical, and financial abuse.

2. The myth that Jewish families are immune to abuse allows both Jewish and secular professionals, including police, mental health professionals and medical personnel, to miss the cues of abuse.

3. Jewish women often either delay seeking help or do not seek help at all. The shame (*shonda*) associated with abuse, the fear of losing their children in custody battles, and the lack of access to financial resources, housing and other needs represent significant barriers for many women.

4. Jewish women do not usually seek emergency shelter and therefore are left alone to negotiate a system of independent and disconnected programs and services.

---

[10] Ibid.

5. Victims and survivors are much more likely to seek help from their intimate network of friends and family members or private psychotherapists than from any other source.

6. Rabbis play an important role in speaking out about domestic abuse.... Jewish women are more likely to go to a rabbi for help and guidance if the rabbi has previously spoken out about the issue.

There is a critical need to address the issue of abuse before marriage. If it is not addressed, another family will suffer. Unfortunately, the topic still remains mostly hidden, though there have been some recent efforts to address the issue of abuse more openly.

In one such attempt, Tasha Joseph, a reporter and writer, created a controversial website in order to list men who cheat on or abuse women. This grassroots effort, which can be seen at www.dontdatehimgirl.com, was designed to help women avoid men who have a history of cruelty toward women. Several thousand men are listed and some women have told me that they have begun to check this site when they get a bad indication about someone they are dating.

■ ■ ■ ■ ■

A seventeen-year-old girl said to me, "The skinniest girls get the best boys." A fourteen-year-old said, "If I allow my dress size to go above size two I might as well just die because I won't have a good future." Although these comments may sound odd or unreal, they are all too common.[11]

---

[11] Goldrich, L. "It's hard to be a body: Eating disorders in the Jewish community." *The New Jersey Jewish Standard,* January 26, 2006.

There has been a distressing increase in eating disorders among teenage girls. Dr. Joshua Lamm has written:

> I receive an alarming number of requests to speak to sixth- and seventh-graders [about eating disorders.] Many of these children have been indoctrinated to fear fat.... They diet, talk about food, calculate calories, compare dress sizes and often feel physically defective.... This group endorses the notion that their obsession is at least partly attributable to their fear of not getting a shidduch. Their mothers or sisters have already warned them of the consequences of eating too much.... They become sitting ducks for the development of anorexia or bulimia.[12]

The indoctrination is so intense that girls as young as twelve have been known to refuse a piece of cake at a party out of fear that they will gain too much weight from just one bite and will become permanently unattractive. The overemphasis on physical appearance also affects young men, who have been developing a compulsive need to "bulk up" in addition to their own expectations of marrying a model whose body appears as if it has been permanently airbrushed.

This overemphasis on physical appearance is so pathological that it cuts to the heart of the tenets of every Jewish family. Most Jewish festivals and events revolve around meals – the sanctification of the event with food and drink. Yet the pressure at these family meals causes so much conflict and ambivalence among young women that for many of them, meals are a time of tension and emotional pain. Some women restrict their diets severely. I have seen women who will eat only carrots and/or soup. Others simply move the food around their plates, putting

---

[12] Ibid.

only small amounts in their mouths. Still others will run to the bathroom midway through the meal in order to regurgitate the food that they have eaten.

The concepts described in Eshet Chayil, where physical beauty is secondary to middot and proper spirituality, are overlooked or completely forgotten in the quest for the perfect shidduch. After all, most of these young women truly believe that if their dress size goes above two, they will not get the best of the wedding prospects for themselves. The sadder part of this belief system is that it is often true because the boys themselves have developed the belief that a prospective date's dress size is her most important attribute. These young men often talk about a girl's "fat potential," a rough indicator of how much weight she will gain once she gets married and begins to have children. Boys, in turn, feel the need to bulk up their muscles in the belief that if they have perfectly-sized, muscular bodies that fit perfectly into thousand-dollar Italian suits with white-on-white barrel-cuffed shirts and gold cufflinks, they will then be more marketable and will have more women flock to them, thus increasing their pool of choices.

How many young Orthodox people are leaving the fold, either gradually or completely? How many are doing so because of the pressures of the dating scene, physical appearance and compulsive behaviors that are not at all relevant to a Jewish lifestyle?

■ ■ ■ ■ ■

Susan returned from her year in seminary in Israel anxious and not well. At the age of nineteen, rapidly approaching twenty, she felt that her opportunities to find the right young man to marry were rapidly fading. She was getting old too quickly, but more importantly, she was able to articulate the fact that the prospective men themselves were too immature. Nevertheless, she felt strongly that she had to marry soon.

In Israel, Susan spoke to her *em ha-bayit* about the pressure she was feeling. The *em ha-bayit* referred Susan to a special *gemach*, which gave her an antidepressant to help calm her down. "I never saw a doctor, but the medicine is helping me," she said. I asked her whether the medicine was actually helping her or was merely getting her through her anxiety over making a mistake.

■ ■ ■ ■ ■

The use of medications both legal, illegal and of questionable legality has soared in this age group prior to marriage. This reflects the intense pressure that these young men and woman are feeling. Young men and women between the ages of eighteen and twenty-five often tell me, "This is a very serious time" and "Dating is serious. We can't have fun. It is just too serious." When asked whether they can be both serious and actually see if they can be friends first, they appeared confused by the question. While we will address the issue of "at-risk" behaviors and their influence on shidduchim later on, this issue of anxiety and the need for outside help, the use of medication or even self-medication that results from the dating scene is part of the crisis.

Whenever Orthodox mental health professionals get together they are careful not to breach confidentiality but they discuss cases that they have been involved in. Some of the more classic ones are the situations where the mother gives her nineteen-year-old daughter Xanax, an anti-anxiety pill, to help her relax and "cope better with the dating process." Mom gets the medication from her own doctor who believes that he is prescribing it to her because she has an anxiety disorder. Mom does not realize that the anti-anxiety medication can, in addition to reducing anxiety, actually be making her daughter more depressed.

Another classic case is that of the twenty-three-year-old woman who is not yet dating but whose nineteen-year-old sister is engaged and whose twenty-one-year-old brother is already married. While the twenty-three-year old woman may be successful at her job or in seminary or college, nevertheless she feels like a "total loser" because her siblings are seen as more successful within the community. So she stays at home most nights and cries bitterly. Sometimes she goes into therapy or is given an anti-depressant. At other times nothing is done for her, so she becomes steadily more depressed and withdrawn. Increasingly, as in the case of the young girl who finds her way to a *gemach,* she manages to get medication by simply describing herself as feeling upset. While this sort of situation is usually limited to closed Chasidic communities, its incidence is spreading.

There has been much discussion regarding the dwindling number of Jews. This is not a new topic. In 1964, *Look* magazine ran a cover story entitled "The Vanishing American Jew." In 1997, *New York* magazine ran a cover story called "Are American Jews Disappearing?" There is some controversy as to how to tabulate the number of Jews in the United States. Questions relate to whether Jews are only those who identify themselves as affiliated or who are culturally members of the tribe.

It appears that in 2004 there were about five million Jews in the U.S. Yet that is the same number of Jews that was reported in the 1950s, when the general population was one hundred fifty million. It has almost doubled since then. As a percentage of the total U.S. population, Jews have gone from about four percent to slightly more than one percent. From this perspective, there is a crisis.

While there has been some controversy regarding the methodology used and the results of the National Jewish Population Survey of 2000–2001,[13] it is abundantly clear that Jews in the United States are marrying later and having fewer children. Also, the intermarriage rate hovers at around 43 percent. A critical note is that this is an overall average. The intermarriage rate for the segment that reports itself as Orthodox is approximately three percent. People leave their religion and intermarry for a variety of reasons.

There is no one specific reason why observant young people look for a spouse outside their own faith. However, many young Orthodox Jews will tell you that at least initially, they date outside their belief group because the pressure is just too intense. What they are referring to is the interrogations that always seem to take place both before and during dating, along with the fear that they may not measure up to some standard that they see as arbitrary and irrelevant. They feel inadequate when faced with an unrealistic formula for acceptance that is impossible for most people to achieve. In their view a date should be a date, not an inquisition. When I meet with individuals who left the fold, even briefly, as a consequence of their dating experiences and I ask them what happened I usually get responses such as the following:

> The shadchan kept setting me up with the same kinds of people. I must have gone out with a hundred speech therapists. That's what the shadchan thought was right for me. I guess there is no one for me in this group.

---

[13] www.ujc.org. Also see: www.simpletorember.com/vitals/WillYourGrandchildrenBeJews.com.htm/. For more general information see the Census Bureau data at www.census.gov.

Why do we have to decide where we are sending our children to yeshiva on our first date?

I may be a woman but I want to be a lawyer. Why does every frum boy I go out with reject me as being too strong or too modern if I want a profession?

Most girls I went out with wanted a learner/earner or just a learner. I am more an earner/learner type so I got rejected a lot.

Aren't religious people supposed to be tolerant and understanding? It feels not like they are trying to do kiruv rechokim [bringing close those who are far away] but as though they are more into richuk kerovim [pushing away those who are close]. And they pushed me away.

It is not just intermarriage that is a concern, but rather marrying out. Many individuals who were raised as Orthodox are marrying out of Orthodoxy finding spouses from other denominations such as Conservative, Reform, Reconstructionist or unaffiliated. There is no data on the percentage of young people who do this, but using the methodology of the Frumstats study cited above I looked at Jdate.com. A good many profiles, perhaps ten to fifteen percent, list "open" as their religious affiliation despite indications of an Orthodox background.

Divorce rates, eating disorders, domestic violence, leaving the fold, fear or unwillingness to make a commitment are all variables that are affected by and, in turn, affect the dating process. Unfortunately, they are not being addressed directly and a crisis has developed.

CHAPTER 2

THE BACKGROUND

THE SHADCHAN WANTED a picture of the girl's grandmother. It seems that knowing the dress sizes of both the girl and her mother was not enough to assure a potential choson [groom] that the girl would not later become heavy because perhaps her mother lost weight for the sake of her daughter's shidduch.

■ ■ ■ ■ ■

The shadchan asked the young man if he wore bobby pins. He was confused by the question. Unsure what she meant and why, he answered, "No." The shadchan told him to turn around and called him a liar, saying, "You are wearing them in your yarmulke." He answered, "You mean my yarmulke clips?" She refused to set him up with the girl she had in mind for him.

■ ■ ■ ■ ■

In the world at large there is a pervasive tendency to treat children as adults and adults as children. Thus, the options of children continually increase as those of adults become more restricted. This yields a situation that produces and reinforces childish adults who always give in to unruly, irresponsible children.

This imbalance extends to the Orthodox community in some significant ways. Often, parents will say that their eighteen- or nineteen-year-old children are not ready for marriage because of a lack of maturity or sense of responsibility even as they hire a shadchan and try to get them married off at an early age. They will also prepare and pay for extravagant weddings and set their children up in fully-furnished homes. Moreover, these married children never need to be concerned about paying the bills. The parents often take care of that even if they cannot afford to do so.

Parents no longer just help out. They take over completely, reinforcing their own and their children's tendencies to ignore real issues. The result is an insidious unwillingness in our community to accept, confront and deal effectively with our challenging communal issues in any helpful way.

The psychological literature calls such behavior cognitive dissonance. This means that we take a cognitive, psychological or emotional position and try to interpret all future information to fit the position that we have assumed even if it does not work out or is not lucid. We continuously attempt to rationalize our view. Ultimately, this leads to an "us versus them" mentality. In this case, rather than acknowledge our shidduch crisis, we point to the dating issues, promiscuity, and divorce in the secular world and tell ourselves smugly that we are better.

There are many factors and variables that distinguish Jews. These include genetic, cultural and ethnic ones that in some important ways make us different from other ethnic, religious or cultural groups. Some of these are minor differences, while others are important to a person's well-being and quality of life. We tend to focus on aspects of ourselves that heighten the positive differences but ignore those that may not be positive. We view our own group as the best and ignore its problems. This is a detrimental way of coping that can result in more difficulties later on.

ANXIETIES

An epidemiological study performed by the National Institute of Mental Health (NIMH)[1] found significant differences between Jewish and non-Jewish samples in terms of specific psychiatric disorders. Jews have higher rates of major depression and dysthymia (less severe but more chronic depression) than Catholics and Protestants. Further studies show that Jewish people experience higher rates of anxiety. Interestingly, although Jews in general are more likely to seek help for these problems than Catholics or Protestants, the data seems to suggest that Orthodox Jews are less likely to seek assistance than members of other religious groups.

The implication of this information is vast and profound. It can go a long way toward explaining many of the issues we currently have and how to begin to correct them. There are several relevant examples.

---

[1] Yeung, P.P., and S. Greenwald. "Jewish Americans and Mental Health: Results of the NIMH Epidemiologic Catchment Area Study." *Social Psychiatry and Psychiatric Epidemiology* 27 (1992): 292–297.
Also see Bonchek, A. "Is OCD A Jewish Disease?" *Jewish Action,* 2004.

The constant fear of parents who send their children to Israel after high school is that their child will "flip out." For them, flipping out means not just becoming more religious and educated within the religion but taking on the trappings or, as one parent put it, "the fetishes" of more religious practice, together with rejecting the parents and the entire lifestyle in which they were raised.

While there is no information as to how often flipping out occurs, there are some anecdotal trends. In a recent case, parents brought a young man to see me because he had "flipped out." At their rabbi's suggestion, the parents brought him to me to evaluate him following a rapid change in his religious beliefs in a short time. In the interview the young man kept returning to a description of his rabbi at the yeshiva he had attended. He painted a picture of a rabbi and educator who was sensitive and warm and set a "beautiful example" of how to live life. It became clear to me that this young man was seeking someone whom he could relate to. Ultimately, he began to describe himself as anxious and with what I believed to be a social phobia.

When I asked his parents, they said that they had suspected for several years that he was always a little too shy and nervous but they were told by his educators not to worry about it because he would outgrow his nervousness. This was the worst possible advice. Not only did he not outgrow his anxiety, but it became steadily worse at the same time that he was learning to hide it more effectively. As a result, he sought out someone who was nurturing and protective. The price he paid was an attraction to an environment that supported his withdrawal from his parents and their desire for him to engage in society. Although they were right to bring him in for evaluation, they were wrong to blame him for flipping out. He was not flipping out, but rather adapting to an anxiety disorder that should have been treated earlier in his life.

I often pose the following question to parents of young men who are in the shidduch scene: "If a boy gets up at four in the morning every morning and sits in the *bet ha-midrash* until midnight every night, what would you consider him to be?" Responses often range from "He must be a real tzaddik" and "He must not need much sleep" to "I feel like he might be a good catch." I am comfortable telling parents that none of these approaches are accurate because I have treated many young men, referred by their perceptive roshei yeshiva, for precisely this type of behavior. Inevitably, they are suffering from an obsessive-compulsive disorder and are often very highly anxious.

In a recent series of articles that appeared in *The Five Towns Jewish Times*,[2] there was a significant debate about whether mixed seating is appropriate at weddings. Some of the letter writers took very strong positions against mixed seating based on their own biases. Other respondents wrote that some of these positions were not supported by halacha or were gross misinterpretations. One brave young woman wrote a letter to the editor describing herself as modern and coming from a modern home. Yet she had attended a wedding where there was mixed seating and had felt uncomfortable. She wrote that her discomfort stemmed not from any halachic reason but from her feeling that several of the young men were looking at her.

My response to such an honest statement is that perhaps she too has some anxiety that needs to be addressed. Is it not appropriate for young men and women who are of dating age to look at one another and, if there is an attraction, to take appropriate action? If the young men who were looking at her were doing so in a socially inappropriate manner, then the responsibility for her anxiety would rest with them.

---

[2] Cf. *The Five Towns Jewish Times,* January–March, 2006.

TROUBLED TEENS AND DATING

I have written about the following issue a great deal (see, for example, *The Jewish Press,* May 19, 2005) and believe it is a factor in the shidduch crisis as well. We have been referring to "at-risk teens" for well over a decade even as we proclaim that the problem does not exist in certain segments of our community and, at the same time, wring our hands over how to deal with it. While many people might claim that we have done much to address the problem, I would say that we have not even begun to deal with it properly.

If we look at the most current research we find that alcohol and substance abuse in the general teen population has been declining over the last seven to ten years. In all parts of our communities, however, the trend appears to be increasing.[3] I also believe that this contributes to the shidduch problem by allowing a large segment of our youth to go untreated and move away from the lives we would like them to have. It also puts a tremendous burden on families trying to hide these troubled teens away so as not to harm other family members who may be seeking a shidduch.

It is important to understand this phenomenon even though on the surface it appears to have little to do with dating. At-risk behavior, which can mean many different things, does not occur in a vacuum but as a part of the family and community in which the teen lives. Virtually every teen labeled "at risk" regardless of how minimally or well adjusted they

---

[3] See Ain, S. "Teen Crisis Detailed in Orthodox Brooklyn." *New York Magazine,* December 20, 1999; Cattan, N. "Orthodox Rehab Programs: Too Much of a Good Thing." *The Forward,* August 17, 2001; Chabin, M. "On Their Own and Using Drugs." *The Jewish Week,* January 28, 2005.

become will feel the effect on whom they date and how they are allowed to find a mate later in their lives.

In order to cope with and correct a problem, it is helpful to begin with the appropriate nomenclature. The title that we have been operating with is incorrect. All teenagers are at risk because almost all teens are risk takers. They think that they are invincible and that rules do not apply to them. Whether the risks they take are small or serious, they are still risks. By not accepting this fact and lumping normal teen risk behavior together with more dangerous problems, we miss the areas that require intervention.

I propose that instead, we use the term "troubled teen" when we refer to teenagers who have significant behavioral, emotional or psychological problems. Not only does it help to clarify the general difficulty, but there is also a large amount of research into children who are troubled, the causes of their difficulties and ways to help treat their problems. If we label it correctly we can then further specify the problem by the type of trouble the teen is in.

Research has shown that four general factors are the root causes for teens that become troubled. These four factors are exposure to trauma; having a learning disability or emotional disorder that is not properly diagnosed and correctly treated; inappropriate parenting; and poor socialization. These factors may be additive or one alone may be sufficient to act as the cause of a teen becoming troubled. The problems also contribute to difficulties with dating and maintaining a marriage.

It is now known that approximately fifteen percent of all individuals exposed to a traumatic event will develop long-term symptoms of Post-Traumatic Stress. The same applies to teenagers who have been exposed to a trauma. One of the telltale signs of Post Traumatic Stress in teens is behavioral or emotional acting out. Exposure to trauma is often random, but at times it may be related to one of the other four factors that cause teens to become troubled. Trauma can occur in many different ways and we need to be prepared to recognize when it happens and intervene to minimize the impact.

While we would all like to believe that our children are born perfect and will remain perfect all their lives, that is not the case. To the degree that we allow ourselves to believe that children perfect or minimize a problem that they may have, we are contributing to the likelihood that they will grow into troubled teens. We do this by refusing to "label" the problem or by creating new programs that are not as intense as those the child may need. It is imperative that we stop reinventing the wheel by starting these "new and exciting" programs that have not been properly researched and evaluated and use the interventions with a proven outcome in order to help children who have these problems.

The third factor, inappropriate parenting, is correlated to all three of the other categories but also stands on its own. Parents can traumatize a child and can be responsible for overlooking, minimizing or inappropriately treating a learning or emotional problem that their child may have. They are also more likely to be simply inconsistent in their parenting. They may threaten to punish a child for an infraction without following through, or they may threaten for no clear reason. They may give mixed messages regularly. Yet perhaps the most dangerous behavior on the part of parents is to allow others to parent for them. They often give the rebbe, teacher, or school the responsibility to parent instead of themselves. In my practice I have seen many parents who want their child's therapist to parent. They will drop off their child before a therapy session and pick them up afterwards, but will not find the time to be a part of the therapy.

No one can take over the role and responsibility of a parent. Children know this instinctively. If teenagers are put in a position where they are exposed to that form of parenting, they will be left without a rudder in a stormy sea. They will also learn to manipulate their environment in very self-destructive ways. They will become needy and demanding and care mostly about themselves.

In our world, we have taken a more highly structured and nuanced approach to teenage social interactions. It has not always been this way, and this change may account for the increase in the number of troubled teens we are seeing. A large amount of research shows that proper socialization, supervised and structured in an age-appropriate manner, acts as a buffer against teenage acting out behaviors. This is something that must be addressed quickly. While there are many programs for teens, only few take into account the need for proper socialization.

Many Jewish communities throughout the United States have used a three-pronged approach to address these four factors. Parents working together with schools and community centers have developed programs to keep their children properly supervised, to provide teens with all the necessary services and to help parents follow through with their responsibilities. Unfortunately, we still approach this with a rigid mind-set, a type of cognitive dissonance that allows us to overlook and, as a result, reinforce negative behaviors that ultimately lead to problems in dating and marriage.

THE TEN DEMANDMENTS

In addition to issues of anxiety we have adopted a parenting style that has been referred to as the Ten Demandments. Parents are not necessarily the demanding ones, but parents have often trained their children to be. Although we are not sure where they originated, these "demandments" describe certain attitudes and behaviors of many young men and women in the shidduch scene, what they are looking for and how they intend to lead their lives. The Ten Demandments are:

1. Thou shalt make me happy. It is always your responsibility to see to it that I am happy.

2. Thou shalt not have any interests other than me. I must be your focus constantly.

3. Thou shalt know what I want and what I feel without me having to express it at any time.

4. Thou shalt return each one of my sacrifices, no matter how minor, with an equal or greater sacrifice.

5. Thou shalt shield me from anxiety, worry, hurt, or any form of pain or discomfort. Therefore, if I am in pain it is always your fault and I have the absolute right to blame you.

6. Thou shalt give me my sense of self worth and esteem.

7. Thou shalt be grateful for everything I do no matter how trivial.

8. Thou shalt never be critical of me, show any anger toward me, or otherwise disapprove of anything I say or do.

9. Thou shalt be so caring and loving that I need never take risks or be vulnerable in any way.

10. Thou shalt love me with thy whole heart, thy whole soul, thy whole mind, and thy whole pocketbook, even if I do not love myself.

Those of us who treat people psychologically or medically or who follow social patterns are not quite sure where these demands came from originally. Although we have modified them somewhat, they indicate a narcissistic approach to life that allows young adults to defer responsibility and create an environment of self-importance and grandiosity. This childish, narcissistic attitude extends beyond the nuclear family to the family that they seek to begin.

If we combine the genetic propensity toward anxiety with an environment that does not deal with the causes of troubled behaviors in teens and a self-importance that borders on narcissism, we begin to find what we see as the background to, or the actual foundation of, the shidduch crisis. By avoiding problems and allowing them to fester and adding an environment that encourages a lack of critical self-examination, we begin to believe that we are the best, that our standards are the only ones that count and that we are entitled to make unrealistic demands of others. In reality, does dress size matter at all? Does using a bobby pin to secure a yarmulke serve as a measure of a person's spiritual standing or quality of middot? Of course not. But if we suffer from an anxiety disorder or develop a phobia about an issue and are subsequently encouraged to believe that our ideas are always valid, then we can justify any position that we may choose to assume. In fact, our anxieties would prevent us from examining our position, no matter how unreasonable it might be.

It is time that we reevaluate the core issues that make up who we are and where we want to be as a society. We need to address the issues of anxiety, depression, and troubled teens in the context of true and scientifically validated intervention, providing the right type of programs for individual, schools and family support and care. Hiding the issue or providing passive programming as an intervention only serves to further promulgate the false notion that it is appropriate to overlook a problem, which actually pushes away even more of our young men and women. Also, we need to move away from the notion that overindulging children, giving them what they want rather than what they truly need, is healthy. Responsible, appropriate parenting beginning at an early age can only help in giving our children a better life later on.

CHAPTER 3

WHO SETS THE STANDARDS?

A PEDIATRICIAN FRIEND recounted a phone call from a shadchan that went something like this:

SHADCHAN: The girl's family wants to know this, and it seems a reasonable question. Can you please tell me if he wears boxers or briefs?

PEDIATRICIAN: I am sorry. Did you ask what type of underwear he wears?

SHADCHAN: Yes.

PEDIATRICIAN: He wears no underwear.

The pediatrician hung up at that point.

■ ■ ■ ■ ■

The shadchan in another situation wanted to know what the girl's mother wore to sleep. It would seem that the young man's family felt this to be an important indicator of her daughter's modesty.

■ ■ ■ ■ ■

In another case the shadchan was preparing the young man for the "perfect girl" for him. She ran through all the proper dating etiquette information and then gave him a pep talk. The one thing the young man recalled as significant was the shadchan's comment, "This girl is so good and undemanding that you won't have to give her pearls in the yichud room. A nice gold necklace is good enough for her."

The shadchan called the young man's parents to find out more about him. All of the information seemed to fit until she asked, "Where is he learning?" "He's in YU," they answered. According to the young man's parents, the shadchan quickly ended the phone call. She called back the next evening and asked a little more optimistically, "In YU, which shiur is he in?"

■ ■ ■ ■ ■

The terms most recently used to describe people in Orthodox circles have been put through such an iterative process that they now serve no function but to describe smaller and smaller segments of society. What does 'modern *machmir*' mean in comparison to 'modern' or 'yeshivish' anyway? While it is true that people in the dating scene are quick to describe themselves in these terms and seem to know what they mean, all that they serve to accomplish is to restrict the dating pool arbitrarily. As a result, the process is divisive and sets up roadblocks to the development of relationships.

Extremism seems to be carrying the day, not just in the radical politics in the Middle East, but in our own community. Who decided that a young man who wears a kippah seruga is less valuable on the dating market than one who wears a black hat? Who determined that what a girl's mother wears to sleep is a reliable indicator of her daughter's character and the type of lifestyle that she will choose for herself? Which *Shulhan Aruch* sets the standard for gifts and how and when to give them? Which scientist has researched the issue of underwear to the degree that it should have any relevance to a healthy shidduch? Yet we have allowed ourselves to be led – even misled – by a small group of individuals who, by employing their own anxiety and compulsivity, now have the power to dictate what have become destructive standards. Unfortunately, many of them have not examined some of their positions to determine their veracity or applicability to our lives. So why do we allow ourselves to follow them?

I am of the strong opinion that religion informs science and science informs religion. I believe in a healthy exchange that allows us to be intellectually honest while increasing our ability to adhere to Halacha and strengthen our beliefs. It is for this reason that I question much of what passes as Halacha or even as religious-scientific fact, particularly in the current climate of divisiveness.

One of my strongest beliefs is that all Jewish people should be tested for diseases such as Tay-Sachs, Canavan's disease, cystic fibrosis, familial dysautonomia and other genetic disorders that are common to the Jewish population. For a very small segment of the population, this idea of genetic testing may have created a reasonable question regarding how to deal with information that may indicate the presence of the gene in oneself or a prospective mate. For most, however, this issue was most frequently dealt with in the past by the potential marital partners and their rabbi or posek.

To help those individuals who understand the importance of genetic testing yet prefer not to know if they are carriers of a genetic disease, an organization, Dor Yesharim, was started. The way this organization operates is to provide genetic testing using a personal identification number. Individuals who are tested by Dor Yesharim receive their own specific identification number. When they find someone they believe they will marry they call the organization with their identification number and their prospective spouse's identification number. The organization will then determine, based on the carrier status of the two people, whether the couple may marry. Thus, if both partners were carriers of, for example, Tay-Sachs disease, Dor Yesharim would not tell them that they are both carriers but would tell them that they should not marry. It is true that if both parents are carriers of Tay-Sachs disease they run a one-in-four risk that every child they have will be born with Tay-Sachs disease. However, the decision process regarding marriage is taken away from the couple and their rav.

While I believe that this process is a reasonable one for some individuals, I think that it creates a series of additional problems for others, primarily the absence of a personal decision-making process. Many poskim do not allow or seriously restrict the testing of a fetus, but there are also many who allow it at certain stages in the fetus's early development. This is a process that should be discussed by a couple in a mature fashion if indeed they are mature enough to marry. They cannot do this if they are unaware of their actual carrier status.

Moreover, and perhaps more relevant to the issue of setting standards, is the issue of intellectual honesty, which is abrogated by this organization. Their flyer[1] states: "Research studies confirm that carrier status knowledge can lead to anxiety, embarrassment, feelings of inferiority and depression." They take this information from an article that appeared in the *Journal of Consulting and Clinical Psychology*.[2] A review of that article indicated that the findings are quite the opposite. What is quoted as fact by the Dor Yesharim pamphlet relates to one study of transitory anxiety that carriers of sickle-cell disease reported. The overall report concluded that there is no standardized study that supports the notion that genetic testing produces any significant psychological distress. Genetic testing should be performed, but according to which standard: an open and honest one or one that removes decisions from the relevant parties?

■ ■ ■ ■ ■

While Suri was at a seminary in Israel for the year, she heard that a new yeshiva would be opening fairly close to her parents' home. While the yeshiva is not Chasidic, one of its policies is that mothers of the boys who attend are discouraged from driving cars. Suri called home and begged her parents to enroll her youngest brother in this new yeshiva. Her reason: she believed that it would help her get a "better shidduch."

---

[1] "Are You or Your Children Dating?" Dor Yeshorim, Brooklyn, NY.

[2] Lerman, C., R.T. Croyle, K.P. Tercyak and H. Hamann. "Genetic Testing: Psychological Aspects and Implications." *Journal of Consulting and Clinical Psychology* 70 (2002): 784–797.

The fact that her mother has had a driver's license and has been driving cars for more than twenty-five years had little effect on Suri. The alleged drive for a "better shidduch" was her main consideration.

■ ■ ■ ■ ■

The drive for more of a "right-wing" approach to life is implicit in the type of behavior that Suri exhibited. Could she actually believe that having a younger sibling in such a yeshiva would allow her to get a better shidduch despite her family's own lifestyle and hashkafa?

While Suri's request is extreme, many others are more commonplace. Some are financial, such as the expectation that parents will support their married children so that the groom can learn without interruption. Interestingly, although many young married men do not want to sit and learn after marriage, they feel compelled to do so because they believe it will help them get a better match.

Many children make social and behavioral demands on their parents as well. Some dictate who their parents may or may not invite for a Shabbos or Yom Tov meal. They decide how their parents should dress; what type of hat the father should wear or whether their mother should wear a fall, a wig or a hat. All of these requests – or demands – display an almost exclusive focus on the façade rather than on the true internal workings of a young couple preparing for marriage. Indeed, so many young people are not ready for marriage that they have a variety of increasing marital and sexual problems and do not even feel comfortable communicating with one another.

Why do we allow ourselves to become something that we are not? Do we truly believe that it makes us more spiritual and religious, or is it just another way of giving into the Ten Demandments? We should be spending our time teaching these young men and women about life instead of acquiescing to a fantasy of how life should be. Ultimately, despite the externals, many of these young married people revert to their prior lifestyles. We gain nothing for them or for ourselves if we do not spend the time teaching them instead of giving in to misplaced haskafa.

A variety of singles events have become available to young women and men seeking to meet and mingle in a more socially relaxed atmosphere. In these settings the pressure of one-on-one dating is diminished. These events are generally geared for people who are considered older, usually above the age of twenty-five, but in some cases, from age twenty-one.

Over the past several years the tradition has developed at these single events that in order for young men and women to communicate, a facilitator, go-between or shadchan, must be present to supervise and conduct the process. These facilitators are usually women who have been married for some time. They are always well-intentioned and supposedly aware of the correct ways to address the different people involved and enhance their meeting and dating experience. At certain singles events, these facilitators actually make the introductions.

If a man becomes interested in a woman or a woman is interested in a man at one of these events, he or she must inform the go-between, who will then decide whether the two should meet and talk. If she believes that they should, she will introduce them to each other. If she feels that they should not, then she will not make the introduction.

I have often wondered how others can make this type of determination when individuals often cannot do so on their own without spending some time together. Further, a passage in the Talmud in Kiddushin 41a states that couples must see each other in order to determine whether they can get along. Also, it goes beyond the realm of basic logic if we allow others to limit the ability to make decisions and then anticipate that these very same couples can learn to become independent and mature. If a couple can date four or five times and then decide that they may not be right for one another but will only inform the shadchan so that the shadchan ends their dating relationship, how can these very same people be expected to learn to compromise, negotiate and accommodate one another in a marriage?

Even more troubling is the fact that in order to attend some of these singles events, one must either pass an interview or be invited. Exclusivity has caused more than one young man and woman to tell me that they will not be involved in a program that promotes a type of "selective breeding." One young woman said that it reminded her "of the cliques in high school, only worse." A young man said that he "would rather go to a club where no one judges you in advance and you can just be yourself."

It has been documented that in certain Chasidic groups, some young men actually faint when they are told what is expected of them sexually on their wedding night.[3] In the Chassidic world the separation of the sexes is an integral part of the cultural mores. Everyone is raised within those standards. The expansion of these standards to all other types of Orthodox religious life has led to a similar marital problem that is increasing. In an article describing what appears to be an escalating phenomenon of unconsummated marriages in the Orthodox world,[4] the authors wrote, "We have concluded that an abysmal lack of basic information regarding sexuality may be the primary contributing cause of failure to consummate the marriage." While the laws of tznius (modesty)

---

[3] Winston, ibid.

[4] Ribner, D.S., and T.Y. Rosenbaum. "Evaluation and Treatment of Unconsummated Marriages among Orthodox Jewish Couples." *Journal of Sex and Marital Therapy* 31 (2005): 341–353.

may prohibit sex education in schools, teaching basic biology is now seen as a religious issue to some. This, combined with a shutting down of any communication between the sexes is leading to an ever-expanding world of difficulty, a disparate set of environments predicated on standards that are simply unrealistic.

The most important questions are: why is this happening? Exactly who sets these standards for dating, for tznius and even for sex education, and why have we allowed events to develop this way? What is the attraction of this approach?

The easiest question to answer is the last one. The attraction is its simplicity and the ability to allow others to set the standard. If others can do that for us, then we do not have to shoulder either responsibility or blame. Much like the parent who wants the rebbe or morah to assume responsibility for a child's ethical rearing, we have given others the responsibility for our cultural and marital standards.

It is always easier to say that something is treif (unkosher) than that it is kosher, and that is the criterion that is currently being used. It is treif if you stack dishes when you clear the table, or if you are a young man who wears the wrong type of yarmulke, and so on. Rather than look for ways to join people together, the benchmark used is the building of artificial walls around people.

I am aware that this is seldom the situation in "out of town" communities. Regardless of one's religious leanings, these communities are mostly cohesive and tolerant. This suggests that insularity is bred by increasingly large communities and leads back to fears or even phobias of the community dwindling. It is also a rejection of the basic Jewish concept "ve-ten chelkenu be-toratecha" – "give us our own unique portion in Your Torah (life)."

Moving away from an inclusive approach sets the stage for these difficulties not only on the larger community level but also on the more idiopathic level, forcing individuals to confine themselves arbitrarily to a tightly-restricted venue. They are thereby exclusionary and have difficulty meeting and mingling with others. It also indicates lack of awareness of some basic psychological principles that enhance life, concepts that we will explore in the next chapter. Knowledge of these principles may serve to help us regain a greater sense of inclusiveness in our community.

CHAPTER 4

PSYCHOLOGICAL PRINCIPLES

THE SHADCHAN SUGGESTED that the young man date a particular young woman, insisting that she was perfect for him. However, when the young man took her on a date he found her a poor communicator, "kind of boring to talk to, and she was at least three inches taller than I am." He refused to speak to that shadchan ever again.

■ ■ ■ ■ ■

The twenty-seven-year-old man is a real catch. He gets up early every morning to learn and afterward works at a well-paying job in a construction firm. Although women had turned him down in the past because of his job, now that he has become a partner in the firm some of them are more willing to go out with him.

Too many, however, cannot seem to be able to get past the fact that he works for a living. For example, one day his car was in the repair shop longer than he had anticipated. He called the woman whom he was to take out that evening and explained the situation, asking whether she would mind if he used one of the company's vehicles. Although she seemed a little hesitant, she agreed.

He showed up that evening in a combination pickup truck and SUV. It was an upscale vehicle and very clean, with a leather interior. He had a good time on the date and felt that she did as well. He was looking forward to another date with her. However, the next day the shadchan told him that the young woman would not go out with him again because of the vehicle. It seemed that she was embarrassed and feared that if they were married, he might drive that car home every once in a while.

People seem to make up their minds very quickly. They have preconceived notions and maintain their positions rigidly despite information to the contrary. Although we may question how they arrive at their decisions, we will not often be successful in changing their minds.

There are some basic psychological principles that appear to dictate how human beings make their decisions. The process of decision-making includes a combination of mathematical, philosophical and logical steps that enhance our ability as rational beings to form our decisions, most often in an unconscious or subconscious fashion.[1] The decision-making

---

[1] For a basic overview see Resnik, M.D. *An Introduction to Decision Theory.* Minneapolis, MN: University of Minnesota Press, 1987.

process extends to many different variables that we encounter in our daily lives and, as we will see in the next two chapters, may even be a primary determinant in the selection of a mate. These principles, which dictate the formation of impressions and how we act on them, include the primacy and recency effects and cognitive dissonance, all of which is subsumed under the study of decision theory.

Decision theory postulates that all people use information that is available to them including their historical experiences, certain preferences,[2] personality and current information to make decisions and form impressions of others.[3] Overall, the way we operate suggests that we give negative information more weight in our initial decision-making process but the process itself is biased by the manner in which we receive the information.

If we respond to information presented initially – that is, if first impressions count more than later impressions do, then we are following the primacy effect.[4] Under the rule of primacy, the theory suggests that we tend to remember the first bit of information presented due to the increased time available for rehearsal of that information. In fact, information presented initially tends to be more influential. This first

---

[2] Betsch, T. "Preference Theory: An Affect-Based Approach to Recurrent Decision-Making." In *The Routines of Decision Making*, edited by Tilmann Betsch and Susanne Habestroh. Mahwah, NJ: Lawrence Erlbaum Associates, 2005.

[3] Krosnick, J.A., and D.F. Alwin. "An Evaluation of Cognitive Theory of Response-Order Effects in Survey Measurement." *Public Opinion Quarterly* 51 (1987): 201–219.

[4] Anderson, N.H. "Primacy Effects in Personality Impression Formation Using a Generalized Order Effect Paradigm." *Journal of Personality and Social Psychology* 34 (1965): 1–9.

impression that we form influences our friendships and relationships because of the impact of the initial positioning of the information.

Although it may seem somewhat paradoxical, information presented most recently, despite the fact that it is more subject to being forgotten due to the shorter exposure time, is also well remembered and carries more weight in our decision-making process. This form of decision-making is based on the concept of the recency effect. Not only do first impressions count, but information that is presented and available most recently is also well recalled.[5] Most importantly, the information that we receive in the middle of the process is not as well recalled, nor do we pay as much attention to it.

In and of themselves, these effects, together with our willingness to accept negative information over positive, have major influence on how we make decisions from the most mundane to the most significant, including whom we choose to marry. They are not the only deciding factors but to a certain degree, our choices are based upon first impressions (the primacy effect) or the last impression, the last person we dated (the recency effect) and whether or not the focus of the information is negative.

The theory of cognitive dissonance[6] suggests that when people are presented with two conflicting ideas about a person, they reduce the dissonance or tension of this conflict in the easiest way possible. In other words, most people tend to rule out contrary information or information that disagrees with their first opinion. This allows the fixing of an attitude

---

[5] Pineno, O., and R.R. Miller. "Primacy and Recency Effects in Extinction and Latent Inhibition: A Selective Review with Implications for Models of Learning." *Behavioural Processes* 69 (2005): 223–235.

[6] Festinger, L. *A Theory of Cognitive Dissonance.* Stanford, CA: Stanford University Press, 1957.

that maintains that the information presented initially is more accurate than any later information, even if that initial information is not necessarily accurate. If one's initial impression is favorable and if one is subsequently provided with information to the contrary, the cognitive dissonance will cause one to reduce the value of the negative information. The converse is also true, as seen in the two anecdotes presented at the beginning of this chapter. If we have made up our minds that a person is not an appropriate match and later information indicates that the person is suitable, the cognitive dissonance will likely be resolved by maintaining the negative view of that person.

Most people tend to make decisions by ruling out negatives, particularly when the decision relates to others.[7] However, this approach is limited because most research strongly suggests that those who look for positives first tend to be more successful in their decision-making. If the approach of seeking negatives first and focusing on them is combined with the primacy effect, the ultimate result is that most of the shidduch dating process tends to rule people out immediately rather than rule them in. This causes a process in which we are more likely to go with our first impression and then remain with that impression in order to reduce any dissonance. The focus is almost always on what may be wrong with the young man or woman even when in reality there is nothing wrong.

---

[7] Cf. Ballantine, M.W. "Decision-Making Processes of Abused Women: The Decision to Leave or Stay. An Application of the Theory of Planned Behavior." *Dissertation Abstracts International,* 4346: 2005. Also see Lind, E.A., L. Kray, and L. Thompson. (2001) "Primacy Effects in Justice Judgements: Testing Predictions from Fairness Heuristic Theory." *Organized Behavioral Human Decision Processes* 2 (2001); 189–210.

Chani decided that she was going to marry only a doctor. She went out with more than forty young men, most of whom were doctors or studying for a medical degree. None met her standards. The confusing thing for her was that at one point in her dating, she realized that some of the men actually were in medical school or were already doctors. Still, they were not what she wanted.

Chani's desire for a doctor is interchangeable with Susan's desire for a full-time learner or Dina's desire for someone who is extremely wealthy or Shelly's desire to live only in New Jersey. All these requirements limit the pool of options and focus on the negative aspect of the decision process – in other words, focusing on a man not as a person but on "what he is unable to give me." This approach sets up a mechanism whereby the first impression is an undesirable one and there is little insight that allows one to go beyond that impression, reevaluate it and allow the focus to switch to the man's positive aspects.

We build first impressions on that negative approach. Basic psychology indicates that we retain the negative view of the person in order to reduce any discomfort that subsequent positive information may offer.[8] This common tendency is exacerbated in the dating scene as we know it, where the pressure to find the perfect person is so intense.

Moreover, in order to overcome the effects of primacy and recency in dating, one would have to date more than one person at a time and attend as many social events as possible. Community members should create appropriate events in order to attract people from the community. This would offer a way to bypass the effects of primacy and recency and

---

[8] Wallisch, P. "Human Mate Choice as the Psychologist Sees It: Findings, Issues, Problems and Perspectives." Available at www.lascap.de.

provide more opportunities to confront and change impressions. Both of these approaches tend to be frowned upon at the present time. Unfortunately, we see that most of the young men and women dating create a fantasy of the perfect mate and have a very difficult time getting beyond it. This is also true for men who reportedly want women of a certain dress size or whose fathers will promise to support them in a certain style until the young man decides that he is willing to start supporting himself.

As we see, the basic psychology of decision-making is significantly exacerbated in the shidduch process. Not only do we allow the focus on first impressions to be a deciding factor, but we also limit opportunities to explore other options in a more open fashion. Virtually no one in the religious dating scene is exposed to what we know scientifically about what makes for a successful marriage.

CHAPTER 5

A SUCCESSFUL MARRIAGE

"My father and my mother
said we'd learn to love each other"

from the song "Do You Love Me?"
from the musical *Fiddler on the Roof* [1]

■ ■ ■ ■ ■

LYRICISTS, DREAMERS AND POETS have been searching for the roots of love for ages and, in turn, how to make a marriage work. The next secret they search for, of course, is that of a successful marriage. Science has also begun to explore effective methods to make a marriage work.

Risa's teacher in seminary gave a lecture to her students about love in marriage. According to Risa, the teacher taught

---

[1] Music by Jerry Bock, lyrics by Sheldon Harnick, book by Joseph Stein. Copyright © 1964.

the young women that the concept of romance in a Jewish marriage is irrelevant. In fact, she was quoted as saying that the boy you date first could just as easily be the right one as anyone else. All that matters is that you have similar hashkofos (outlooks on life). Although love can develop afterwards, it is not necessary for a good marriage.

According to the growing body of scientific evidence Risa's teacher is wrong, so wrong that it may actually explain the growing divorce trends we are seeing. I often see young women in their early twenties who are extremely anxious about meeting the right man. All they want is someone who "will grow spiritually." When I ask them what that means to them they often cannot articulate a clear response. Frequently their response is, "You know what I mean." When I push for a more detailed response I find that they are referring to a vague notion of what religious life should be like based on an image that they have been exposed to again and again without truly understanding how it applies to them. When I point out research that indicates that individuals raised with a religious background tend to become more spiritual as they age,[2] that it is in fact anticipated, they are universally shocked. They almost never talk about themselves or what they may need or, who they may actually be and how they define themselves.

---

[2] Hunsberger, B. "Religion, Age, Life Satisfaction, and Perceived Sources of Religiousness: A Study of Older Persons." *Journal of Gerontology* 40 (1985): 615–620.

PERSONALITY COMPATIBILITY

It is becoming increasingly clear that people who have personality profiles[3] that are more alike are more likely to be compatible. Using what has become known as the "Big Five" personality factors, profile similarity measurement uses these five factors – agreeableness, conscientiousness, extroversion, neuroticism and openness, to develop profiles of personality and compatibility. In fact, the more alike the partners' personalities are, the likelier they are to grow together and have a satisfying relationship.

Many studies that have examined partner-compatibility predictors have found that the more alike the couple is at the beginning of the relationship, the stronger and more loving the relationship will become over time. In one study of the emotional compatibility of sixty couples who were dating, the authors concluded that in those relationships where the two partners' emotional patterns were similar at the start, the likelihood of the relationship's success was greatly increased as measured by increased cohesiveness and significantly reduced likelihood of separation.[4] An interesting sub-finding of the same study indicated that the more alike these individuals were at the outset, the more alike they would continue to grow over time. This is especially true of emotional reactions. The couples that were more alike at the outset of their dating

---

[3] For a complete overview of how to assess personality profile similarity see: Salamon, M.J. "Every Pot Has a Cover: Finding the Right Personality Relationship Fit." University Press of America (2008).

[4] Zentner, M.R. "Ideal Mate Personality Concepts and Compatibility in Close Relationships: A Longitudinal Analysis." *Journal of Personality and Social Psychology* 89 (2005): 242–256.

tended to laugh and cry at the same things more frequently with the passage of time.

There appears to be an innate process at work in the matching of personality profiles. Another study reported that couples are much more likely to be satisfied in their relationships and significantly less likely to separate when both partners' personality profiles match the traits that they see as ideal.[5] These findings were confirmed in both a theoretical study of approximately sixty students and a considerably larger study of two hundred ninety-one people who were in relationships. The researchers reported that positive associations between similarity of the couples (that is, the more alike they were), their degree of attachment and personality profile congruence were strong predictors of marital satisfaction.[6] There is even some research that explains this phenomenon. One series of studies found that people are more attracted to others who are like themselves in any number of ways, even including arbitrarily assigned code numbers that mimicked other subject's birthdays, because it unconsciously activated a positive association about themselves.[7] Of

---

[5] Asendorpf, J.B., and S. Wilpers. "Personality Effects on Social Relationships." *Journal of Personality and Social Psychology* 74 (1998): 1531–1544; Klohnen, E.C. and Shanhong, L. "Interpersonal Attraction and Personality: What Is Attractive-Self-Similarity, Ideal Similarity Complementarity or Attachment Security?" *Journal of Personality and Social Psychology* 85 (2003): 709–722.

[6] Shanhong, L., and E.C. Klohnen. (2005) "Assortative Mating and Marital Quality in Newlyweds: A Couple-Centered Approach." *Journal of Personality and Social Psychology* 88 (2005): 304–326.

[7] Jones, J.T., B.W. Pelham, M. Carvallo and M.C. Mirenberg. "How Do I Love Thee? Let Me Count the Js: Implicit Egotism and Interpersonal Attraction." *Journal of Personality and Social Psychology* 87 (2004): 665–683.

course, while superficial attractors do not keep relationships going, personality profile and emotional similarity are not superficial attractors.

One interesting report of five experimental studies indicates that physical attractiveness may affect the selection of a mate in a very interesting fashion. What the report concluded was that both men and women attended to physically attractive females, but when they were limited in their ability to see them, only the men developed biased views of attractiveness while the women did not.[8] This can be interpreted to mean that men who are not allowed to interact with women tend to develop biases as to how an attractive woman is supposed to look. Therefore, they are probably more likely to be increasingly demanding and unrealistic in their descriptions of what they see as beauty.

Indeed, what all these studies strongly suggest is that similarity, especially of personality and its subcategories such as emotion, contribute to compatibility. Furthermore, spending time to allow the determination of whether two people have that similarity actually improves success rates in relationships.

Further research provides even more insight into the process of falling and staying in love. In fact, neurochemical changes occur in the brain when people fall in love.[9] In a study using MRI brain scans, people who were "madly in love" were shown a picture of their loved one or a neutral picture. When they were shown the neutral picture, the MRI scan

[8] Maner, J.K., D.T. Kenrick, D.V. Becker, A.W. Delton, B. Hofer, C.J. Wilbur and S.L. Neuberg. "Sexually Selective Cognition: Beauty Captures the Mind of The Beholder." *Journal of Personality and Social Psychology* 85 (2003): 1107–1120.

[9] Fisher, Helen. *Why We Love: The Nature and Chemistry of Romantic Love*. New York, NY: Henry Holt, 2004; Gonzaga, G.C., R.A. Turner, D. Keltner, B. Campos and M. Altmus. "Romantic Love and Sexual Desire in Close Relationships." *Emotion* 6 (2006): 163–179.

recorded no changes in their brains. However, when shown a picture of their beloved, the parts of the brain most often linked with a sense of pleasure lit up. These areas, the ventral tegmental area and especially the caudate nucleus, are the primary location for the neurochemical transmitter dopamine, which is one of the chemical messengers in the brain. Its specific function is the triggering of an intense rush of pleasure, and research shows that it has the same effect as cocaine. The neurotransmitter dopamine makes you have a sense of elation, sleeplessness, and excitement. It also helps you become more alert and focus more intently on things. On the other hand, dopamine is also related to psychosis and movement disorders such as Parkinson's disease, so a constant flow, either too much or too little, of dopamine may not be good. Instead, what appears to happen is that during the first two years of a loving relationship, dopamine is more likely to be released. After that time the neurotransmitters serotonin and oxytocin, known as calming or mood-stabilizing chemicals and chemicals that help humans form bonds with others, tend to take over. In fact, time spent together may mediate the brain's production of these neurotransmitters. The more time spent together the greater the brain's output of these chemicals.

Sociological studies of marital happiness may actually confirm many of the research findings from brain chemistry and psychology. For many years sociologists have reported that a U-shaped curve describes marital happiness. At the outset of a marriage and in the first few years, most couples report a high degree of marital satisfaction. When children are born the level of reported happiness declines, but when they move out, it recovers. More recent, statistically sophisticated studies, however, show that the bliss reported in the first few years of marriage declines but likely stays at the stabilized level.[10] It is also reasonable to assume that if the level of happiness is higher than average at the outset of marriage, the stabilized level will remain higher throughout the marriage.

Thus far we have seen that we all use a similar decision-making process. If we alter the process to rule in positives rather than rule out negatives and allow ourselves to be open to dissonant ideas rather than stick with first impressions, we are more likely to make better decisions. We have also seen that personality similarity is a strong indicator of marital happiness and success and seems to have a clear biochemical basis.

Knowing oneself is clearly an important component in the process of finding a mate. The ability to determine degree of similarity in personality may be an unconscious process. Yet the degree of knowing what that similarity means for you and how you want it to proceed is a critical factor in finding the right mate. Many young people have begun to believe that they should limit their dating until they are absolutely certain that they are ready to get married. This approach limits their ability to gain experience by making decisions and exploring what is truly attractive. This does not imply that dating should begin at any specific age, but rather suggests that the rigid approach to dating with only the intent of quickly finding the right mate and getting married rapidly may not be the most effective method of guaranteeing marital happiness.

---

[10] Van Laningham, J., D.R. Johnson, and P. Amato. "Marital Happiness, Marital Duration, and the U-Shaped Curve: Evidence from a Five-Wave Panel Study." *Social Forces* 79 (2001): 1313–1341; Umberson, D., D.A. Williams, M.D. Chen and A.M. Campbell. "As Good as It Gets? A Life Course Perspective on Marital Quality." *Social Forces* 84 (2005): 493–511.

"I know my bashert [intended mate] will somehow come to me." The young woman was so convinced that if the shadchan called and the man described did not meet the requirements of her list, she would not accept the date, retorting, "Why waste time?" That was her position at age nineteen and it continued until she was twenty-six years old.

At that point, when most of her friends were already married and some had already had their second child, she changed her tune. "I realize that finding a bashert requires effort. I hope I didn't miss my chance."

Too often, the idea of a *bashert* contributes to a passive attitude toward dating. The notion of *bashert* is misinterpreted to mean that somehow the right one will appear magically and there will be no need to see if indeed that person and you are similar and attracted to one another.

The concept of *bashert* seems to originate in the Talmud (*Sanhedrin* 22a) where it is written: "Forty days before development of the fetus, a Heavenly voice declares that the daughter of So-and-so will marry So-and-so." Too many people interpret this to mean that a perfect mate will be available automatically. Yet at least two other Talmudic sources force us to reevaluate what the term *bashert* means. Does it mean that the perfect mate will be our *bashert?* That is not likely, because in BT *Yevamot* 63b Rav Yehuda, the same Rav Yehuda who in Tractate *Sanhedrin* stated that a voice announces who will marry whom, told his son: "The verse in Kohelet, 'I find woman more bitter than death,' applies to your mother." Although she may have been Rav Yehuda's *bashert,* she was clearly not his perfect match. Is it possible to lose a *bashert?* Yes, according to Tractate *Moed Katan* 18b, which allows a marriage to take place on the intermediate days of a festival lest a partner lose an intended spouse.

It appears that the Rambam, at the beginning of the eighth chapter of *Shemonah Perakim,* completely rejects the notion of *bashert.*[11] In *Igros Kodesh* (vol. 2, 193) the Lubavitcher Rebbe, quoting the Rambam, indicates that while there may be an inclination toward someone who is *bashert,* there is also a need to exercise free will. According to this line of reasoning, free will allows us the opportunity to seek out the best mate so as to fulfill the mitzvot of marriage properly. As mentioned above, the Talmud in *Kiddushin* 41a speaks out strongly against arranged marriages and requires that prospective mates meet in order to determine their compatibility. Rashi even states that a messenger may be sent to choose the bride, deliver the marriage contract and betroth her, but only if the man cannot go himself. If he can go by himself but chooses not to, in Rashi's opinion he has committed a transgression. Rav Moshe Feinstein also indicated in his *Igrot Moshe* (14:1b) that if a man finds a woman attractive, with a solid background and of a proper religious level, then he should not probe further to determine whether she is his *bashert.* He wrote that the couple should marry with hope and the belief that they are intended for one another. Also, Rav Soloveitchik said, "One cannot form a friendship unless he finds in it the realization of a value long cherished by him" (54).[12] Clearly Chazal recognized how vital the process of meeting, dating and getting to know one another is for selecting the most compatible mate.

There is a clear mandate here for choosing someone using a healthy decision-making process. As discussed above, this includes choosing someone with a similar personality and then seeing if there is chemistry

---

[11] Also see *Teshuvos ha-Rambam,* siman 159.

[12] Soloveitchik, J.B. *Family Redeemed: Essays on Family Relationships.* New York: The Toras HoRav Foundation, 2000.

between the couple as well. This approach has nothing to do with questions such as "Does the family keep the garbage in a can in the open or is it hidden in a cabinet?" On the contrary. As Rav Soloveitchik said, "Besides physical attraction, husband and wife must feel friendship for each other" (54).[13] In other words, the attraction must be deeper than the physical and must be part of a personal, emotional and personality bond.

---

[13] Ibid.

CHAPTER 6

THE WAY WE ARE

THE SHADCHAN WAS attempting to introduce a woman to a man who insisted on knowing whether the woman was "put together." After thinking for a second, the shadchan answered, "She is not put together but she comes with easy-to-assemble instructions. And if you have any leftover parts, you can pass them along to the next guy."

■ ■ ■ ■ ■

I see many young men and women in my practice just before they start dating, while they are dating and soon after marriage. While many of them are deeply involved in many activities such as yeshiva, seminary, college and chessed projects, too many of them have no connection to anything meaningful in their lives. Though they go through their days doing what is expected of them, they are essentially building their resumes rather than connecting emotionally or spiritually to the very activities that take up their time. They are only connected to their lists, which consist of their desires and fantasies, which in turn demand that the person they ultimately become serious with think and behave in a very specific way. This behavior is formulaic, mechanistic and, very often, superficial.

I hear many men say things like: "I want a woman who does not wear denim skirts." Or: "Her skirts should never have a slit." Then there is the man who wants the woman to be "a lot more religious than I am so that she can get me to do the right things." "I want a woman who doesn't care if I wear a tee-shirt." For their part, the women want "someone who knows how to buy the right gifts." Or: "He can work only if it doesn't interfere with his learning." What is not stated but implied in this last comment is "even if there is desperate financial need."

At present our world is based on lists. Lists of attributes – girls want tall guys, guys want thin girls, lists of middot: "She has to be warm and sensitive because so few girls are that way today." "If he doesn't relate well (immediately) to my parents then that's a sign." There are even lists of clothing styles or tablecloths that are acceptable. Yet none of these lists are helpful to finding a proper mate and often they are destructive. A beautiful woman who will wear only woolen skirts may have a nasty disposition. A tall man who wants to learn may turn out to be a cruel spouse. A list that includes the question "Are your grandmother and grandfather buried next to each other?" provides us with no useful information about a prospective mate.

Perhaps the most destructive of the items on our lists is what one singles web site describes as the "Orthodox observance list." What these items characterize is the alleged various philosophies that define religious belief systems today. I have reviewed several web sites and researched these categories and find that there can be from seven to thirteen or fourteen categories to which people assign themselves. While these *hashkafot* (philosophies) supposedly help classify the type of mate one is searching for, in reality they are little more than a front for factionalism. Review with me some of these categories and let us see how confusing, reductive and divisive they truly are.

The Modern Orthodox category is an interesting one. Originally only one category, now it is two – liberal and *machmir*. The liberal categorization is defined by some as Orthodox Jews who observe the laws of kashrut and Shabbat but are more "relaxed" about other aspects of Halacha. One site states that a common form of behavior among this group is that they are open to secular activities including bars, clubs and movies. Using this definition, some would classify all troubled teens and those with a history of having been troubled as fitting in this category. However, troubled teens and adults can be found in every category. Another site defines "modern" as a category in which men might not wear a yarmulke in public and women might wear trousers or not cover their hair.

According to the Orthodox observance scheme, *machmir* moderns are stricter in their religious observance. The differentiation between this category and yeshivish modern, which is apparently the next level of strict observance, is that modern Orthodox *machmir* are not yeshivish, which means that they probably did not attend the right Yeshiva. Interestingly, the combining of clubs, bars and movies is also arbitrary in several ways. Going to the movies is not the same as going to a club. Ask anyone who has spent any time in a club and in a movie theatre how many yeshivish people they have seen in either place, and you will see how absurd these criteria are.

The next category is yeshivish. Here too there has been a split, resulting in yeshivish modern and yeshivish black hat. The difference between yeshivish modern and yeshivish black hat apparently has to do with working. The more modern ones work, usually at full-time jobs. Someone once explained to me the difference between a Yeshiva

University (YU) type of man and a yeshivish modern and yeshivish black hat man this way: "If a YU graduate is an attorney he will dress in a blue suit with a striped shirt and wear a yarmulke at work. If he is yeshivish modern, he will always wear a black suit and white shirt but no yarmulke at work. A yeshivish black hat will be an attorney but will be full time in the kollel." The implication of the statement is that the YU graduate wears his religion like a flag on his head. The yeshivish modern also wears his religion but as a clothing statement. He does not wear a yarmulke just in case he is put in a compromising position between Halacha and the secular legal system. The yeshivish black hat man spends his time in the bet midrash rather than at a secular job. This generalization highlights some of the false and frankly insulting implications of this system of categories.

Next we get into chassidish. Here, too, there seem to be at least two categories: chasidish modern and chassidish. Here too, the modern category represents those who work, while those who are not modern learn full-time. Beyond these two general categories there are, of course, the various types of Chasidim such as Satmar, Belz, Breslover, Lubavitch and so on. Some Chassidim use the "Bashow" system of meeting. In this system the two meet in a home and do not date outside. This is a specific type of meeting style where dating, as discussed in this text, is irrelevant.

In addition, there are the categories of shemirat mitzvot that are supposedly designed for observant Jews who do not want to be pigeonholed because they do not believe in these categories as well as Litvish, *dati le'umi* (national religious) and Haredi *dati le'umi*. The last two supposedly represent Israeli classifications that are somewhat similar to Modern Orthodox and Yeshivish respectively. Haredi Dati Le'umi is also a Zionist group, though it is yeshivish.

There is also the Carlebachian category, which represents individuals who are followers of the late Rabbi Shlomo Carlebach. While observant, they are reportedly relaxed in their observance but more spiritual than the modern orthodox category. Then there is the category known as "hafifnik," which supposedly describes people who are "half and half" in their observance but haven't decided yet where they will be in the end. Finally there is the category of "I'll tell you later," which I believe may include people who want to marry a Jew but may not be Jewish. In my research I have seen some profiles of young men who list themselves as "I'll tell you later" whom I personally know. Some of them are from Orthodox backgrounds, while others whom I recognize live in predominantly Jewish neighborhoods but are not Jewish themselves.

Those who use these categories often cite disclaimers that they are not and should not be used to make judgments about people. Yet isn't that exactly what they do? They also state that using these criteria is essential for choosing a spouse because similar attitudes towards religion and levels of observance are essential for compatibility. In my many years of research, I have never seen any indication that this is valid. In fact, I have never come across any research supporting any of these limiting and discordant categories. On the contrary, as we have seen in the chapters above, similarities in personality, emotionality and the ability to have choices in selecting a mate are the most important factors in finding the right spouse.

Yet the dating public is given an overabundance of categories with a paucity of useful information. With a little creativity we could probably add more to this *reductio ad absurdum*. In fact, many young women do precisely that when they add statements like they would like a learner, an earner, a learner/earner or an earner/learner.

Some historical data may inform our discussion further. In Europe, people usually did not ask questions regarding category of observance. They asked, "Where do you come from?" Though many jokes were made about it, Hungarians married Poles and Russians married

Czechoslovakians. The pictures from the towns they lived in included people who wore hats together with those who did not. Families had chassidish members as well as more modern members. Shadchanim did not label people so that they would be restricted to arbitrary categories.

In Israel today are many families that also run the gamut. I know of one family with sons who are emotionally connected and supportive in spite of their very different hashkafot. One son is a rebbe in a "black hat" yeshiva while another is a rebbe in a hesder yeshiva, which would be roughly equivalent to modern orthodox in the US. Still another son became a Chassid who learns half days and works half days, and a fourth son became a physician. In another family of my acquaintance, one son studies in kollel, another is a movie producer and a third is a paramedic. In these families there is no question of belonging, *hashkafa* or observance. Everyone belongs equally. Each family member is supportive of the others' choices, and all are equally observant.

In my search for any data that would be informative for today's dating society and that would support the notion of these observance categories, I have only found criticism of them. Nevertheless, they are being used without any understanding of their destructiveness. A web site entitled www.NerdTests.com has a survey called "The Orthodoxy Test." It is clear from the questions – and I also believe – that the test was designed as a way to poke fun at the absurdity of these categories. After completing the test it computes into which Orthodox observance category one fits. I have heard from many young people between the ages of seventeen and twenty-one that they consulted the test seriously to see where they might fit.

The test questions include items such as "Higher secular education is…" and "Being *machmir* is…." Responses range from the extreme to the extremely absurd. Take, for example, the question that starts: "Yeshiva University is…." The response options are a) a makom tumah; b) frum, but just barely; c) acceptable, although a little leftish, d) a good example of a centrist normal orthodoxy, and so forth. I chose this question partly because it shows to a very large degree the stereotyping and *lashon ha-ra* that is taking place. Is there a YU type? If you believe there is, then you have never been there. At YU you can find any type of Jew, often in abundance. I mentioned this question to a friend who is a rosh yeshiva in a chassidish yeshiva. He answered that aside from the obvious *lashon ha-ra* of the concept, that there are plenty of good Jews at Yeshiva University and many of them learn better there than at other more *"yichusdik"* yeshivas.

Another question on the test is also instructive. "If the Rambam (Maimonides) were alive today he'd be…." Response choices include a) Right wing yeshivish b) Left wing yeshivish c) Right wing modern orthodox d) left wing modern orthodox e) considered an apikores. The gist of this question goes to the heart of the issue that the Rambam worked as a physician in addition to his many writings on Halacha and hashkafa. But a statement that I hear very often – "We don't pasken that way" – characterizes the larger issue. It has become an excuse to limit, omit and degrade anyone that we see as different. I have heard it applied to Rav Samson Raphael Hirsch as well as Reb Chaim Volozhin. What does this categorization process accomplish beyond producing artificial boundaries? The creators of the test are sensitive to this and, through humor, poke fun at the meaningless categories. Yet sadly, the humor is lost to many who believe that reasons do exist for these foolish groupings.

■ ■ ■ ■ ■

The Internet has become a primary source of, and a vicarious cyber-support group for, all types of people with all kinds of needs. People who are dating or about to start dating are no exception, and they can choose from an almost infinite number of Internet sites to have all types of discussions. The Internet is anonymous and anyone can find support, right or wrong, for almost any position with just a few clicks of the mouse.

Even in the Orthodox world, there is an overabundance of dating sites, weblogs (or "blogs"), discussion sites and web forums. Some of these forums have names such as Hashkafa.com or Frumteens.com. A review of some of the postings to these forums suggest that there are some very appropriate and relevant topics being discussed but there are also many confused and misdirected people who use these sites as clearinghouses for information. It is instructive to study these sites in order to develop an understanding of what people seek and what they believe.

On one such site a young woman asks:

> Where can I find a shadchan who specializes in someone who would accept me? I am a BY (Bais Yaakov – i.e., yeshivish) girl but my mother doesn't cover her hair and she sometimes wears pants in public. Is it possible to find a man for me who will accept my parents and their lifestyle even though I am not like them?

Another one asks: "Is it possible to live a life where one can go to the movies but not have a television in the house? I am dating someone who wants to do that and it seems hypocritical." Responses run the gamut from "Don't worry; it will all work out" for the first question to "You can't live in two worlds. You have a serious problem and need to fix it quickly" for the second one. While the first response is actually realistic and quite supportive, the second is destructive. The anonymous respondent is imposing his rigid belief system on someone who is not required to follow those beliefs.

One interesting post on another site went something like this: "I have tried to find a relationship the 'goyishe' way, by falling in love. It hasn't worked. Now, I want a Torah-based relationship. I have no idea what it will be like to get married to someone I am not head over heels about."

Perhaps I missed the shiur that day, but I am quite certain that it is not against Torah principles to marry the person you love. As we saw before, love actually develops along with a chemical reaction brought on by similarities and compatibility between the two people. One response to this person's posting was close to accurate. The respondent wrote: "It is possible to have love and a Torah-based relationship. It requires a period of practicality to determine whether values, character and goals match. After that you can rationally allow the relationship to go to a head-over-heels level. This way it can be both practical and loving." Other respondents espoused only one or the other approach such as "Look for love first and foremost" or "Love is irrelevant. Torah principles dictate the best marriage partner."

Another poster asked whether others have had experiences similar to hers. She is nineteen years old and has not had any positive experiences with a shadchan. She writes:

> They treat me like just another piece of paper. They say things or make me feel like they will look out for me but there are so many older girls who are seeking out the same type of man. It feels like one big unfair competition. Even if you don't use a shadchan and just ask family or friends they also seem to be looking out for themselves or their other relatives.

One respondent misled the young woman by writing, "All you have now are your prayers, money and the stuff that will get you noticed. Dating more guys is not helpful. Cry your heart out to Hashem and your *bashert* will come to you." While no one would reject the idea that prayer is helpful, is it not misleading to believe that prayer alone will turn a person's dating life around? Isn't it incumbent upon the person to go out and do the work to find the right mate, even if it is difficult? It is indeed difficult, and becoming harder still.

On one site someone posted an article with a title often used on dating web sites, "Relax and Date." This article, however, is a personal questioning of the shidduch scene. Perhaps it is even a bit of a rallying cry in that it states rather boldly, in capital letters, "Relax and Meet People." The author, who is apparently a woman even though identifying information was deleted, laments the fact that dating in the present scene amounts to a catch-22. If you meet someone appropriate in the grocery, at work or at school and he asks you out, she advises her reader to say yes. But "of course the good guys wouldn't ask the girls out because they're not supposed to, so if one does he isn't a good guy, so a good girl would never say yes." She goes on to question whether this rigidity is to ensure that couples are *shomer negiah*. She responds that "If a couple wanted, they could do stuff while dating. Those who don't (choose not to) are following Halacha. It's ridiculous to infantalize adults." The cynicism of the article comes out in the last few sentences where the author supports the notion of the rules requiring the arbitrary separation of the sexes. She writes that without these rules, "you have the disintegration of Orthodox Jewish society."

These are some of the responses she received: One writes, "I totally agree with you. Someone should remove these artificial barriers." Another writes, "I think it's absurd that religious people set up obstacles to meeting other religious people. Why shouldn't singles meet in shul, at a

Shabbat table, in a religious neighborhood? What better way for religious people to meet each other?"

However, the majority of responses were like this one. "My question is this: if you feel this way, there are religious Jews who do believe in meeting in a non-shidduch (or at least not only via a shidduch) atmosphere: the modern Orthodox. It seems like you agree with them more. So why not just join them?"

Herein lies the problem. If you are in the dating scene, you are categorized and forced to take sides. As we saw above, there are several possible causes for this divisiveness. But the scene itself is perpetuating it.

The shadchan scene appears to be predicated on a few principles. First among them is the acquisition of information. As we have seen, questions asked can be general or specific and range from reasonable to absurd. One site geared to helping the shidduch process states that the shadchan should "Ask general questions... so as to promote useful answers." These questions should include "What level is his learning?" "How far down do her dresses go?" or "Tell me about the person's mental or physical health." The shadchan is then instructed to get specific precise answers rather than generalizations or value judgments.

The site goes on to suggest that asking as many questions from as many people as possible about a prospective shidduch is very appropriate. "The more people you speak to, the more likely you are to uncover inconsistencies, fabrications and meaningful data."

Two obvious problems here are the author's own contradictions. In the first case the examples are anything but general questions. They may not be as specific as "Can he learn Tosafos?" or "Are her skirts always mid-calf or longer?" but the questions he suggests require a level of specificity that, as we have seen, is highly irrelevant. Again, as they did in Europe, perhaps the best type of question would be "Where is he or she from?" This is a general question and would give us enough information to gain some picture of the person and the influence of his or her environment. It would also be in line with the recommendations of the Chafetz Chaim, as we have seen above.

The other difficulty is that too much information can be misleading and wrong. We have known for a long time that thinking too much can be distracting and cause us to make the wrong decisions.[1] That is why students are often instructed on standardized tests to review their choices but not to change their mind once it is made up. Inevitably, when an answer is changed it is wrong. We also know that the influence of a person's impression is affected by the way in which the information is presented and includes a variety of non-verbal information as well.[2] When we ask various people about a potential mate, we will merely receive each individual's biased response. True, if there is a convergence of information that can paint a picture of the person that could be very useful, but it is highly unusual and also very unlikely.

Therefore, those who wish to be part of the shidduch scene are left with the options of a shadchan, a shidduch club serving as a shadchan, or Internet dating, with or without a shadchan. All of these approaches draw information that may not be useful and then channel it in ways that may be not only non-productive but also negative. In addition to surveying informants about a specific potential shidduch, matchmakers and shidduch clubs, together with some dating sites, attempt to acquire information about their clients using questionnaires. A review of some of theses "shidduch application forms" indicates more of the same.

---

[1] Wilson, T.D. and J.W. Schooler. "Thinking Too Much: Introspection Can Reduce the Quality of Preferences and Decisions." *Journal of Personality and Social Psychology* 60 (1991): 181–192.

[2] Betsch, Tilmann, and Susanne Haberstroh, eds. *Preference Theory: An Affect-Based Approach to Decision-Making.* Mahwah, NJ: Lawrence Erlbaum Associates, 2005.

Questions always include "Do you consider yourself a) Chassidic b) Yeshivish c) Modern, etc" "What will you use to cover your hair?" "What are your father's and mother's occupations?" "Do you go to movies?" "Do you attend shiurim?" "What do you enjoy doing in your spare time? a) learning, b) reading, c) sports, d) arts and crafts, and so on," and "Please write three to five words that describe you." Again, we are dealing with reductivism, bypassing the fact that the best way to make choices is by having the dating options available for a direct evaluation. What results from these incorrect approaches are profiles that are often superficial, dates that are disappointing and even marriages that may fail.

Many Internet dating sites cater specifically to Jewish people. They include such well-known sites as Jdate.com, Frumster.com and SawyouatSinai.com. They also include Jewishcafe.com, thejewishpeople.com, jsoulmate.com, jewishdate.com and Dosidate.com. Jlove.com, organized by OnlySimchas.com is designed to cater to Orthodox Jewish professionals, the majority of whom are over age thirty. There are many more, as well as some that are being developed and updated with increased specificity such as Matzahmate.com, which caters to modern Orthodox and Conservative Jews or those who would not mind dating a Conservative Jew. There is also a site called Jretrodate.com, which caters to people who will only date through a shadchan, hence the "retro" part.

People who use these sites provide all of their information by self-report in response to the web site's questionnaire. They also include pictures of themselves at most sites. Very few, if any, information about the participants is verified, though there are courses for people who choose to date by this method on how to develop a "glowing" or "stellar" dating profile. Many of the profiles are earnest attempts to portray oneself in the best possible way in order to attract the "perfect match." Still, many of the profiles are inaccurate, laughable or worse.

Some pictures are obviously dated. Some pictures of the women are from dress-up affairs, while others are deliberately too casual. In one profile, a man in his early thirties wrote as a description of himself: "I am a control freak." Another thirty-year-old man wrote, "I want someone who will help me take care of my mother." One woman who gave her age as twenty-five wrote that she was looking for a Prince Charming who would understand her need to live "very near my parents." Another woman wrote that her primary interests included "Kiruv and sharing good divrei Torah," but did not mention what she was looking for in a spouse.

The examples are endless, which is a positive thing. It shows that there actually is someone out there for everyone. Unfortunately, the profiles are often so sparse and misleading that they make it difficult to decipher whether or not there may be a real opportunity for a serious date or not. Moreover, even in those sites that try to focus on personality there is perhaps only one that employs a valid scientific method in order to assess the respondent's personality. This site, Jewishtypes.org, uses a personality assessment tool to match personality types. Most other sites rely primarily on an individual's self-written profile. While some profiles may be honest and accurate, not all are. I have heard of several instances where people post false information on dating sites as a spoof. Finally, even where the information is accurate and a potential date exists, web sites do not provide ways for a couple to spend time together.

There is clearly a vested interest in continuing these varied forms of shidduch dating despite their difficulties. To overcome these difficulties would require an honest evaluation of the entire system from the way we expect the potential mates to behave to allowing a more realistic approach to meeting and dating to a loosening of the power of the shadchan who rejects the reality of proper behavior in dating couples.

CHAPTER 7

A MATURE DATE

THE WOMAN STARTED her conversation with me by saying:

> In 1981, just before I got married, my father said that I
> should make sure that I was good friends with my intended
> mate because, in his words, "The big love doesn't last
> forever." My mother said that before I became half of a
> couple I should make sure that I was one whole person. My
> daughter got married last year and she wouldn't listen to any
> advice I had. Her concerns were only about his philosophy
> of life and long-term goals.

This woman's parents gave her excellent advice. It is impossible to
know the causes for her disagreements with her daughter, which may be
due to the Ten Demandments lifestyle discussed above. Nevertheless, I
often hear parents in the Orthodox world complain that when it comes
to dating advice, their children rarely approach them anymore. Rather,

they are much more likely to get advice from their teachers, shadchanim or dating books.

I have reviewed many of the books written to help guide people in their serious dating efforts and analyzed other sources of advice for daters in the general population. I have discovered that most of the advice given falls into seven categories. The following review excludes those categories that pertain to aspects of dating that are not halachically relevant.

The first category is one that I call *Preparation*. Dating advisors always advise that those who would like to be successful in the dating process must first make the commitment to dating. This includes being prepared for excitement, letdowns and pain, and having the right frame of mind to do the work that the following categories require.

I call the next category *Looks*. Almost all advice about dating suggests that you have to allow yourself to look good. Some suggest starting an exercise program or trying a new hairstyle or diet. By itself, these recommended changes are mostly superficial except that taking care of your looks always leads to a strengthening of your level of confidence, which is the next category.

Confidence is a critical component for success at dating. In addition to working on oneself physically, one can build confidence by avoiding people who are negative about their lives or dating experiences. It can also be built by spending time in an environment where you can be with supportive, understanding people who challenge you to keep trying harder.

Category four I call *Advice about the Time Frame*. If you see yourself dating with the goal of getting married in two years, then you have to approach the dating process differently than someone who wants to get married within a year or, conversely, has no time frame whatsoever. If you have no time frame then you have to determine what the ultimate goal of your dating is.

The fifth category is *Realistic Choices*. Daters are instructed to be realistic about the people they date. Are they at the same level in terms of personality, looks and life goals? Daters are advised that if they end up dating someone who is emotionally different or whose appearance differs from set expectations and level of comfort, they should be prepared for some problems with the dating process.

Meeting is the next category in this scheme. Most specialists advise prospective daters to find the best spots to meet people. These can be societies, houses of worship, supermarkets, sports clubs or any other place where people can meet. Even on-line dating sites make this recommendation despite the fact that it may draw business away from the site.

The final category in this scheme is *Enjoyment*. People are advised to enjoy the process of dating. Dating is designed simply as a way to meet people and socialize. The most realistic way to find the right person, according to this conceptualization, is by meeting as many people as possible and coming across the right one in the process. Daters are also confronted with the need to take a short break from the process every once in a while to recharge their confidence batteries.

These seven groups of suggestions are by no means comprehensive, definitive or a guarantee of success in dating. Nevertheless, they make certain assumptions about people who are going to be dating. The first is that they are serious about the dating process. The second is that they have achieved a certain level of maturity that serious daters should have. Finally, they must be willing to take a critical view of themselves and make the changes necessary to improve and succeed.

I have also reviewed several shidduch books and some of the advice given is similar to the categories described above. The primary differences relate not to being serious about dating – the shidduch scene requires seriousness and even demands it – but to the level of maturity and willingness to look within and make changes if necessary. It seems that many shidduch books are written at so basic a level that they do not assume the minimal level of maturity necessary to date. Nor, in many cases, do they assume the introspective aspect either. Many books actually offer a script on how to conduct the first phone call or the pros and cons of where to go on a first date. Some have a checklist on how to prepare for dates. To be fair, many of the books written for the general population provide specific suggestions for date preparation, but virtually none are as detailed as the advice given in shidduch advice and dating books.

In the shidduch texts, recommendations for men include: brush hat, wash hair, trim beard, make sure shirt has no stains on it, tie matches suit and suit fits, no holes in socks, wallet is stocked with at least one hundred dollars, don't forget where you parked your car, and so on.

For women, the checklist is not much more mature. It includes: shower (apparently only men need to wash their hair), brush hair, apply makeup, take along some cash, listen to the weather and prepare appropriate clothing, prepare clothing at least a day in advance, make sure clothing is clean and pressed, and so on.

I may be wrong, but as I said above, most if not all of these items should be part of an adolescent's repertoire of self-care. Are we encouraging adolescents to date or are we infantalizing adults? If they need this much help in preparing for dates, should they be dating? Can they make decisions that will affect their lives if they have to be told to shower or brush their hair or have some money in their wallets when they go out on a date?

Virtually all shidduch books recommend that immediately following the first date both parties report to the shadchan to tell them how that date went. The shadchan will contact the people in turn to let them know if both want to continue dating. If either one of the parties choose not to continue dating at any point, they are instructed to notify the shadchan, family member or friend who made the connection so that they can end the dating relationship. This cannot be construed as a sign of responsibility or independence. If they are at the age where they are to make such a momentous decision, why must these couples be prevented from dealing directly with one another?

Although I have no one specific answer for these questions, a comment from a young woman can be instructive. She said:

> I was married at the age of twenty and divorced just before my twenty-first birthday. Everyone thought we would be perfect for each other. My parents and his parents got along wonderfully. My mother asked what I thought about him, but he was everything on my list that I wanted so that's what I told her. He was a good person but we had nothing in common except our lists. I was told by the shadchan that he was perfect for me and we could make a nice life together but there was really nothing between us. Our match was made based on superficial similarity and availability, not compatibility.

Who made the decision for marriage in the case of the young woman above? One could argue that it was exclusively her fault. One can also argue that it was both her own and her husband's fault or the shadchan's fault for minimizing the woman's concerns. The best argument, however, is that the decision was taken away from the young woman not just by the shadchan, but also by the lists and the parents' limited input. Decision-making is not based on the individual's emotions, feelings or insight but on the system's expectations. When we remove the ability to decide from someone, we infantilize that person. Perhaps couples are so infantilized and babied in the hope that it will strengthen their relationship. Maybe parents protect young couples because they are worried that the subsequent marriage will not work out. If, as mentioned at the beginning of this chapter, parents are not consulted when it comes to dating, then protecting their children from pain can be a strong motivator. Unfortunately, there are several flaws in this approach that reinforce the cycle, permitting children to have ever-increasing options while gaining too much power, leaving parents who are disempowered with the ultimate result of rearing childish adults. This is yet another variation of the Ten Demandments.

In order to break this cycle, a serious attempt to bring the dating scene to a more mature level is required. We need to bring dating back to its original definition: simply the process of meeting people. The long-term goal of dating is meeting the right person to marry. We have to stop confusing the definition with the goal. When young men and women begin dating, they are led to confuse the definition with the process. Historians of marriage such as Stephanie Coontz have reported that a form of dating referred to as "calling," which is most similar to the shidduch dating of today, was very popular among the general population in the late 1880s. But it lasted only until the 1920s because it severely limited options for meeting and dating.

We must allow people to date in a way that reduces the immediate pressure of marriage and increases opportunities to meet people. The long-term goal is the establishment of healthy, solid, committed relationships. This would require a variety of changes that would not take too long to institute but will take major effort.

CHAPTER 8

A GAME PLAN

THE FATHER OF A twenty-three-year-old woman said to me: "How very typical and now how so very rare. I met my wife at a Purim chagiga twenty-five years ago. Our children don't have that option. My neighbor's sister called the other day with a boy for my twenty-one-year-old daughter. He sounded fine until the woman said that he wants to learn full-time for four years and either I or my daughter would have to commit to support him for that amount of time. When I told the woman that I couldn't afford to support another family and that my daughter would probably not agree to his terms, the woman argued with me. She said that my daughter is getting old and that if she doesn't seriously consider these terms she will probably never find a good mate."

While the father did not believe that his daughter would never find someone, he was concerned that she might develop a bad reputation as someone difficult to date. He was perplexed and very upset and tried to speak with his daughter about the phone call. He was sure that the woman's prediction of doom was not accurate but wondered if his daughter was too picky in choosing a spouse or, conversely, would she take what the shadchan said as Torah from Sinai and jump into the very next dating relationship that came her way, no matter how inappropriate it might be. Initially his daughter was reluctant to discuss the matter at all. After speaking with someone she called her "spiritual advisor" she told her father that while she understood his concerns, in the future she would go out with anyone who might be even slightly appropriate.

While her agreement to date is a positive decision, unfortunately the motivation comes from the wrong source. The pressures to conform to this increasingly manipulative system can only result in an outcome where there is a greater likelihood of errors. This twenty-one-year-old woman, like most people in this scene, does not have the option to meet men on her own but must go out with men based on lists of attributes and well-intentioned but coercive outsiders.

Dr. Allison Conner of the Cognitive Therapy Associates once compiled a list of the top dating mistakes.[1] The shidduch system seems to be developing in such a way that five of the mistakes are actually built into the process. They are: (1) *Game-playing* – playing it cool, not getting too involved, manipulating; simply put – not being honest about what you need.

(2) *Obsessing over details* – worrying about who said what and how it was perceived, giving in to irrelevant details and not looking at the overall picture of compatibility.

(3) *Interrogating your date* – This is most often done by the shadchan but also by the date. All the questions described previously, together with a

---

[1] www.cognitive-therapy-associates.com/top-ten-dating-mistakes.php

host of equally irrelevant, reductive, and divisive questions, place too much pressure too soon in the dating process. A "wrong" answer often means denying the couple time to actually discover if they may be right for one another.

(4) *Not being honest about your needs* – Pretending, or trying to force yourself to believe that everything will be all right in the relationship because he or she fits the list requirements of physical size or shape, type of hat or dress, how the Shabbat table is set and so forth, but not the personality requirements necessary for a real relationship.

(5) *Sacrificing too much to get the relationship* – Accepting aspects of her or his personality that really grate on you in an attempt to force a relationship even when it becomes clear that a relationship cannot exist.

These dating mistakes can be avoided with some minor changes and some major effort on the part of those who are dating and their parents. Below, I will tell parents and daters how they can begin to make these changes.

PARENTS

The greatest error parents make when it comes to childrearing at any age is the assumptions they make about their children. The worst assumption is that they know their children well. I have found that many children are left to their own devices because parents are either too busy or are too disinterested to deal with their children. This issue is a developmental one that needs to be addressed from the time children are born until they become mature enough to care for themselves. While the shidduch process often distresses parents, they feel completely disempowered to become involved. To do so requires that parents follow some basic steps, some of which begin early in their children's lives.

Simply put, many parents do not know their children well enough starting at an early age. As a result, children may be left to their own devices while their parents can only follow the lead that their children set, even to the point of watching them make the wrong choice of spouse or lifestyle.

Parents must *know their children.* In order to do that, I suggest that parents communicate extensively with them. Perhaps the best way is to follow the rules of journalism by becoming involved and asking such questions as who, what, when, where, why and how. In order to understand your child properly, you must be able to answer the following questions:

Who? There are two components to this question: who are your children and with whom do they spend their time? The first part requires a real attempt to understand your child's personality. To do so entails spending time with your children and allowing them to show their true interests, abilities, skills and special talents. It is not fair to force a child who is adept at mathematics but not sufficiently coordinated to play basketball to spend hours on the court. Perhaps a math or chess club is what the child needs. If the child has an interest in sports, then a wise parent will encourage that interest realistically.

Similarly, a wise parent will not force a child who has limited ability or no interest in learning to spend many years in the bet midrash just for the sake of a good shidduch. Nor would parents who have been asking the right questions wonder about who is influencing their child once he or she begins the dating process.

The second component of this question is to know with whom your children spend their time, with whom they are the most comfortable. Parents can gain tremendous insight regarding their children's social skills and the personality types to which they are attracted and with which they feel comfortable when they pay careful attention to this part of the question.

What? – This is an all-encompassing question that applies to almost all aspects of your child's life. What is your child doing? What does he or she enjoy doing? What motivates him or her? What is his or her learning style? What is his or her socialization style? What is his or her pattern of rest and leisure? The point of this question is to understand the range of the child's behaviors, temperament and personality because most of these patterns continue throughout their lives. It will also provide evidence of what may be changed and what must be accepted in the child's basic personality style as he or she becomes an adult. These questions also provide insight into areas of concern, particularly as that child wants to begin dating. What kind of life does he or she seek? What makes him or her anxious in this process of meeting people?

When? – This question is specific to temperament and particular actions. When is the child going to react to certain things and in what way? When will the reaction abate? When will the child want to engage in another behavior? and so forth. Regarding behavior specifically, the question has to do with the primary issue of when to allow the child to be with certain friends and for how long. This component is a critical one in preventing teens who take risks from becoming troubled. If parents know with whom their children will be and when, they can have better control of some of these situations. Parents can also prevent some acting-out behaviors and channel their children more effectively, even to the point of assisting them with the dating process.

Where? – Where is the child most comfortable? Where does he or she like to be? Where is his or her comfort level? In teens this aspect is significant. Parents should know where their children are, not only whom they are with. Too often, when teenagers are dropped off at someone's home or an appropriate program, they may not remain there. "Where are you going and with whom?" are important buffers that protect the child not just from dangerous impulses but also from any influence that parents may have cause to question. In the dating scene, this goes beyond asking where your child is going on a date. Parents should be asking: Where are you going to meet people? Where is this relationship going?

Why? – When children are very young, they are forever asking "Why?" "Why is the sky blue?" "Why do I have to read?" "Why do crickets make noise?" And so on. Parents almost never ask why, but they should. "Why do you want to go there?" "Why do you like this teacher?" "Why is this homework so interesting to you?" A world of valuable information can be obtained from children throughout their lives if parents would only ask them why. The applicability to dating is obvious: "Why do you like or dislike this person? Why do you think it can or cannot work out? Why are you accepting a date with this person?" or "Why won't you go out with him (or her) again?"

How? – The significance of this question increases as the child passes through the teen years into adulthood. Questions such as: "How do you plan on accomplishing that?" have particular relevance to serious dating. "How do you plan to live your life? How do you plan to finance your life? How do you see it working out?" All of these questions are relevant to understanding children and their needs and helping them find ways to set and accomplish their life goals.

If parents spent the time and asked the questions, they would know their children a great deal better. Getting to know their children instead of turning a blind eye to their needs means getting them help if and when it should become necessary. Parents who overlook, minimize or deny that their child may have a learning problem or a behavioral, psychological, emotional or socialization issue only help to make the child's problem worse.

Parents often overlook their children's problems out of a fear that if they acknowledge the problem it will have a negative influence on the child's or a sibling's shidduch. Other parents overlook or do not address issues because they allow themselves to believe that others such as teachers, rebbes or other leaders are caring for their child. Unfortunately, this leads to a cycle of disenfranchisement for the child, who fears a lack of acceptance or ultimately feels totally rejected. In turn, this can only lead to a worsening of the child's problems, making the hope for effective treatment that much dimmer.

Yet if parents know their child and learn how to advocate on his or her behalf, they can work to find the resources necessary to get that child help when he or she needs it, regardless of his or her age. I believe that if parents did this, there would be less likelihood of teens becoming troubled and troubled teens having difficulty with dating. As we discussed above, Jews are prone to mood and anxiety disorders, the symptoms of which can become evident at very early ages. If parents invest the time in asking the right questions and being with the child, the proper form of treatment can be made available.

■ ■ ■ ■ ■

Parents' responsibility goes beyond knowing their child to include *knowing their mentors.* It is far too easy for parents to abrogate their responsibility to care for their child to a responsible surrogate, often the rebbe or teacher. Fortunately, children can benefit from having another caring adult watching and teaching them. Yet unfortunately, rabbis and teachers are responsible for many children and while they do have an interest in their charges, their interest is limited by the amount of time available to them divided by the number of children for whom they are responsible. Moreover, while parents want their children to expand their horizons, the rebbe's or teacher's hashkafa (philosophy) may be, and often is, different from the parent's to a greater or lesser extent. This difference can lead to significant problems when it comes to the shidduch process and the wedding.

Human beings form belief systems in various ways and at different ages. If a young woman in seminary hears a statement such as "The first boy you go out with is probably your bashert" and her parents say nothing to the contrary, she may make the wrong choice for a husband. If a young man's rebbe tells him, "You must spend the next four years after your wedding only learning" even if the young man is unwilling or incapable or his family cannot afford it, he may also make the wrong decision without proper parental input.

Too often children's mentors overlook issues that their pupils may have. While a teacher's advice – "Don't worry; she'll outgrow it" – may soothe a parent's concern, it may still be wrong and carry long-term implications.

■ ■ ■ ■ ■

Know your child. Know his or her mentors, and *stay involved and be realistic*. This is the third component of parenting to help your child through the shidduch process. If parents raise their children in an environment where they are encouraged to communicate and respond to questions; if parents have been involved and had input together with their children's mentors, then they are halfway there.

Although the task is difficult, it is rewarding. In one sense it is excruciatingly complex because it requires parents to acknowledge that while their children will remain their children forever, they are attempting to become mature adults, and to allow their children to continue to that next stage of development. At the same time it requires that parents act as advisers and negotiators, something that children entering the dating process may not realize that they need and may not want.

This stage requires the parent to ask the right questions, provide the right advice and not give in to a child's demand for something that may be inappropriate. I am reminded of a nineteen-year-old boy, still in yeshiva and just starting college, who demanded that his parents allow him to marry a young woman he had met only two months before, buy and furnish a house for him and support him and his wife until he finished college and decided what he wants to do.

Even if parents can afford such an enormous commitment, there is good reason for them not to consent. It is also imperative that when parents make a commitment to assist their children either financially or in some other way, that they provide the assistance in a realistic manner. In particular, while some parents want to help and will support their children during their first year or two of marriage, they must have contingencies in place in case of financial setbacks. These are important issues that need to be discussed. The attempt to shield children from them and remove them from the reality of the situation can only lead to conflict.

Parents must also act as the shoulder to cry on if their children should find that dating is not going precisely the way they had envisioned it. They must also be prepared to prod their children to change their approach to dating when necessary. Moreover, parents need to assist their children in negotiating the stages when a relationship becomes serious. Parents can deal with all of these tasks far better if they have been involved with their children from the beginning and remain realistically involved as they enter the dating process.

DATERS

A happy marriage is among the most important safeguards we can have as we deal with life's stressors. People who report being happily married tend to be healthier, wealthier and more satisfied with their lives than single people do. When searching for a marriage partner, we often confuse a happy marriage with superficial compatibility. Yet the ability to argue does not correlate with marital happiness. Having a fight does not matter; rather the way in which a couple resolves their conflicts has a significant effect on their happiness. Couples who work together to resolve quarrels and who do positive things for each other tend to have better marriages. We must strive to have a plan for dating that seeks ways to match according to these abilities rather than focus on superficial traits or behaviors.

KNOW YOURSELF

One of the most important things that daters can do for themselves is to throw away their shidduch list. Such lists are superficial and provide almost no insight into what makes a good match. The list that daters should keep is one of themselves – their own needs, traits and personalities. Such a list will help you get to *know yourself.* We cannot expect to find the right spouse if we cannot define who we are. It is the height of deceitfulness if we have a list of what we want from others but have no insight into ourselves.

As we have seen, the best predictor for success in relationships is similarity – of personality, emotional tone and personal outlook. Knowing whether a person will grow spiritually – as if there were a way to know the future! – or whether he or she is yeshivish modern or black hat does little to determine compatibility. Externals change, often very rapidly. Internal traits, such as personality, tend to change little and last a lifetime.

If you need to make a list, make it consist of who you are. Make that list short on superficial traits and long on personality, character and emotions. What makes you happy? Are you quick to show emotion? What causes that emotional reaction? Are you an anxious person or a calm one? Are you extraverted or introverted? Do you enjoy trying new things? Are you agreeable by nature? Once you have your list of who you are, you can start to find someone who is compatible with you.

There is good reason for the fact that William Shakespeare's line from *Hamlet*, "To thine own self be true," has been famous for centuries. If we are not true to ourselves, if we seek someone who we think will change us or complement our weaknesses, we are more likely to have a difficult time. True, it is good to have someone to help us when we need help and whom we can help when that should become necessary. We all search for relationships that provide support, but this cannot be the primary goal of marriage.

Those who marry with the goal of changing their spouses or being changed by them are often disappointed. If we are anxious by nature, we may need an understanding partner. On the other hand, we may have a hard time with a partner who is never anxious because that person will have difficulty understanding our reactivity. The same rule applies to all personality traits. Of course, this does not mean that we must find someone who is perfectly compatible based on a reliable and valid personality test. It does mean that we should have similar profiles regarding many of the same traits and reactions so that our compatibility will be enhanced.

To know ourselves also means that we must acknowledge other aspects of our needs in a relationship. We cannot marry someone whom we find unattractive because our own definition of attractiveness is the one that should count. Another person's definition of attractiveness should not apply for us. Adopting someone else's notion of acceptable height or weight distracts from the true connection that we wish to build.

The issue of lifestyle choice causes a great deal of friction in relationships these days. Deciding as a couple to become a member of a Young Israel or an Agudah shul should not be a major cause of conflict. While there may be perfectly good reasons to join either one or even another shul entirely, those reasons should not lead to conflicts about overall philosophies of life, certainly not during the first few dates. The couple, not outsiders, should make the decision. While it is important to try to find the right place for our own hashkafa, it is at least as important to learn to compromise and accommodate in order to develop a deeper, healthier relationship.

REALISTIC LIMITS

People who are ready to date for marriage must learn to *set their own realistic limits*. Dating is not based upon a strict recipe. It should not be left to a formula that dictates: "If nothing is happening by the third date, it's time to call the shadchan to end it." Conversely, the formula that says "It's the twelfth date, so I must make up my mind immediately" is also not realistic. Remember that the process of dating is a process of meeting and getting to know people. There is much truth to the notion that we can get to know someone quite well within the first few minutes. Yet we should not rush in making a commitment to spend the rest of our lives with that person. If we are honest with ourselves, we will know whether the person and time are right.

Dating also raises the specters of pressure and fear in many people. It is a process that can seem like a roller-coaster ride. Even people who enjoy the ride's jolting ascents and descents and high speed need to take a break from the action every so often, especially if things are not progressing in the way they would like them to progress. Taking a break should not be seen as a sign of failure. On the contrary, it is display of a willingness to reevaluate one's needs and thus a sign of maturity. If you are in the process of dating and are feeling too pressured, take time to explore the cause of that anxiety and find better ways to cope with it.

Another form of anxiety common to dating is performance anxiety or stage fright. One young man told me that he was so nervous about a date with someone who was described as a "totally perfect person whom I would fall in love with immediately. They said that she was so perfect for me that I got so nervous that I stood her up." He simply did not show up for their date. Stage fright is common, understandable and, at times, even useful. It helps us put our best foot forward because it causes us to increase our awareness of a situation. Entertainers report that a healthy amount of stage fright helps them prepare for a show and that without it, they are often not as involved in the performance as they should be. Yet if the level of anxiety is too high, then it would be wise to seek help in order to determine the causes and ways to deal with it. Avoiding stage fright or performance anxiety, pretending that it does not exist or overreacting to it may only exacerbate one's fears, making the pursuit of a relationship that much more difficult.

SOCIALIZATION

Whenever I mention the following suggestion, I immediately hear a chorus of boos from shadchanim. Rather than see this as a negative position against the use of a shadchan, I see this as a way to expand the shadchan's usefulness. Rather than using lists of items that focus on availability, I challenge all those involved in this process to move to compatibility as a method of matchmaking and employ it in larger group formats. Here is my specific recommendation: in addition to, or perhaps instead of working exclusively with one shadchan or particular shidduch club, get involved in *social activities*. These activities, which are often community-based, are part of a larger organization that can extend the networking capability of any single person or limited group. The more social exposure we have, the more likely we are to find a temperamentally similar, compatible partner. Nevertheless, make sure it is an activity you enjoy. If it is not, you will simply be going through the motions and you will become increasingly frustrated.

As we have seen, when we meet someone, our preconceptions, personality and moods affect our decision-making process. We also know that comparing our options can, and often does, lead us to making more appropriate choices. This is hard to do when dating is exclusively sequential, when we date one person after another; where comparison is based on recollections that may be biased or on pressure from others who insist, "She is perfect for you."

At a lecture I gave, one woman told me that social programs "tend to be a place for wild and unhealthy behavior." That is a terribly biased and unfair misconception. Not only are people trying to date for the purpose of marriage, but they are also entering into a new, more mature stage of life. This phase requires people to be more open to socialization and dealing with life's realities. If we are not capable of acting appropriately, then we might be tempted to behave in a wild and unhealthy way. Yet if we are prepared to move on to the next phase of life, then we will behave correctly.

Socializing also means that we do not miss opportunities to meet people, whether it means going to the supermarket or walking to shul on Shabbos. All we need is to let ourselves act in a way that allows us to be approachable. Too many young people of marriageable age walk the streets with their heads down or pretend not to see others or, worse, do not even respond when someone greets them. All of these things are not only signs of poor middot but also missed opportunities.

Socialization allows for a more natural way of acting. In a dating situation, the pressure of the one-on-one date is removed. The ability to interact should be enhanced because of the freedom to interact with many people. Being able to communicate directly, without a facilitator or shadchan, is a much more mature and realistic way for people to determine how well suited they may be for one another. Remember, *Kiddushin* 41a insists that prospective partners meet one another so that they can see whether they will get along. This insistence is based on the Torah precept "Love your neighbor as yourself" (Leviticus 19:18). It is hard to communicate with someone, let alone love someone, if we do not communicate directly on our own. When we reach the age of decision, we must learn how to make decisions. Although the process may be difficult, it can only be enhanced if we start to do so for ourselves.

While dating more than one person at a time may seem taboo, there is no Halachic reason not to. If we are dating for the serious purpose of marriage and we are aware of how decisions are made, then we can see why it may be sensible at times to date more than one person at a time.

We are all social beings. We belong to social groups and attend social events. The process of finding our true match should – must – include this process of socializing. To exclude it makes for a very stilted and grueling process that contributes to our acting at times without understanding all of our needs and how to meet them in the marital relationship.

In order for the social contract to operate properly, there must be honesty. Honesty in dating includes presenting ourselves in an honest fashion and communicating honestly. Maturity dictates that we deal openly and directly with our dates. If the relationship grows into a marriage, we have already begun to build a strong foundation with that honest approach.

If one of the parties wishes to end the dating relationship, then honesty and maturity require an open, if brief, discussion as to why. So many people have told me that they just wanted a reason why the other person did not want to continue dating. "Was it something I did?" "Is there something wrong with the way I present myself?" Telling a shadchan, "We just aren't growing" is at best evasive and unfair. Of course, we need not be brutally honest if we find someone unattractive or totally incompatible, but we can say, "We don't seem to have similar approaches to life," "We have different personalities," "You seem too strong a person for me" or even "I think you are a great person but we don't get along well enough." Honesty counts for a lot in life. Do not sell yourself short by taking shortcuts with it.

FINANCIAL REALITIES

A word about finances is in order. No relationship, outside of a business relationship, should be formed based on finances. Much too often people will make statements like "This match is for you because the family has lots of money" or "Her father's business is big enough to accommodate you whenever you are ready."

An even worse example is the following:

> We were going out for over two months. The relationship was terrific. We were able to relate to one another and understand one another and there was something special happening between us. He went home and told his parents and I told mine. He called me two days later and we met. He was crying. His mother said that she had checked us out and

112

he had to break it off with me because my family didn't have enough money to support him.

A general rule to live by in marriage is that money is not the primary issue; maintaining and improving the relationship is. One item that couples fight about most often is money and it is one of the primary causes for divorce.[2] Often, these financial problems are related to poor fiscal management or even gambling. Yet just as often, financial reversals can cause significant marital discord if it is one of the components upon which the marriage is built. Simply put, we cannot marry for money or the promise of an easy life that money may bring. It is not realistic to believe that the current levels of funds available will always exist, nor is it sensible to try to predict a future life based on the stock market. Conversely, many people marry with the attitude that money does not matter at all. This too, is the wrong approach to a marriage's success. Still others have set a price for acquiring the right type of marital partner.[3]

A young woman may truly believe that she would be proud to work full-time while her husband studies in kollel. While in many cases that is a desirable approach, unfortunately, I have often heard women say, after having been in this position for several years and having three or four children, "This is not really what I anticipated." They experience disillusionment when their husbands do not contribute to their family's economic welfare.

---

2 Amato, P.R., and S.J. Rogers. "A Longitudinal Study of Marital Problems and Subsequent Divorce." *Journal of Marriage and the Family* 59 (1997): 612–624. Hetherington, E.M., and J. Kelly. *For Better or for Worse: Divorce Reconsidered.* New York, NY: W.W. Norton, 2002.

3 Levinson, Chaim. "How Much Would You Pay for a Groom?" Ynetnews.com, January 14, 2007.

Some studies of families in which the husband did not work but the wife did showed a shift of dominance from the husband to the wife. Under these circumstances, women made most of the economic decisions and then ultimately dominated other aspects of the marriage. The impact of this on a husband's sense of self can be staggering, especially if he sees his wife as too domineering. If a wife says that she is "tired of him not accomplishing" while he feels that he is, the grounds on which the marriage is built become very shaky.

Similarly, parents who support their married children completely for a long time may also have a negative impact on the couple's sense of self-esteem. The effect can be pervasive, as in the case of young marrieds who become totally dependent on others and irresponsible regarding financial issues. Regardless of how successful the married children may become in their own right, if their parents support them completely, they will almost always develop a pervasive insecurity and haughtiness in order to overcompensate for their poor self-esteem. This can threaten the well-being of the marriage and the well-being of both partners in other social interactions.

Couples who build their relationships on a variety of factors that include emotion, personality and love, rather than on finances or attitudes that promulgate divisiveness, are much more likely to have marriages that grow.

VIOLENCE

There are indicators of people with behaviors that should be avoided. As mentioned above, domestic violence exists in all communities. Being aware of the signs early on may prevent a bad relationship from developing.

Not all people raised in abusive households are themselves going to become abusive. A history of abuse by itself is not a strong indicator. The best indicators are behaviors observed while dating. As a general rule, if someone makes you feel uncomfortable because he or she are too strong, too pushy, or too intense about the relationship too soon in the dating relationship, do not feel obligated to continue dating him or her. Even if the person professes an immediate love for you, this type of intensity too soon may bode ill for a relationship.

While the following list is not all-encompassing, it includes important indicators of serious trouble. One should avoid dating:

- The woman who insists on ordering food for you at the restaurant even if she has never been there before

- The woman who insists on spending all the time you share with her exclusively with her family

- The man who refuses to meet your friends

- The man who ignores your successes or is quick to trivialize your work or your ideas

- The woman who always makes disparaging remarks about you to your friends or family

- The man who agrees to spend time with your friends but is much too flirty with them

- The man who gets angry too quickly and remains angry for an extended period of time

- The man who has quick flashes of temper and throws things or yells at the drop of a hat

- The woman who becomes jealous much too quickly, or is much too controlling

- The man or woman who calls you names – obviously not ones of affection or endearment

If the person you are dating exhibits any of these or similar behaviors, it may be time to get out of the dating relationship as quickly as possible.

ONLINE DATING

Those who use an online dating forum to meet people should be aware of several points. Online dating can often be a cold-hearted, confusing and bewildering process. If you are going to use an online dating service, use ones like eHarmony.com or Match.com, which employ algorithms and personality tests to make matches. The human third-party bias factor is removed in these online services, allowing the focus to be on people as they present themselves in reliable tests of personality.

The two sites I mentioned are the largest and rapidly growing sites for dating in the general population, claiming as many as ten thousand or more new subscribers every day. The reason that they are so large is because of their continuing efforts to use a scientific approach to dating, which seems to work quite well. Matches are made based on mathematical formulas, which seek comparable personality profiles. The most successful users of these sites tend to be older individuals or those who have dated for a long time and not been successful with more traditional approaches.[4]

Younger individuals – that is, below the age of thirty – are starting to use online dating sites more frequently. The beauty of online dating is that it allows the comparison of several individuals, thus limiting the primacy and recency effects. Some sites also allow an individual to date more than one person at a time or at least date one at a time and keep a few others on "hold" until a decision is made. Still, it is important to match based on personality, emotion and other compatibility factors, which many online sites do not perform.

Groucho Marx said, "Marriage is a wonderful institution. But who wants to live in an institution?" Marriage should be a warm, loving, supportive, nurturing environment where both partners grow together throughout their lives despite life's troubles. This can only happen if we make an effort to go beyond the institutionalized divisiveness that we see today in the dating world to an environment that supports growth through experience and finding the right mate. In order to do this, we must acknowledge our problems and work on them. We must also become aware of the best ways to deal with our own issues rather than someone else's ideas of who we are.

While we should be open to others' input, we should not use it as our only guide. Let us throw away our lists. Let us stop overlooking or hiding family problems. Let us not accept abuse. Most important, let us know ourselves, our personalities and our emotional makeup.

---

[4] Egan, J. "Love in the Time of No Time." *The New York Times,* November 23, 2003. Keeler, G. "Happily Ever After... Internet Love." *The Fresno Bee,* February 13, 2005.

APPENDICES

APPENDIX I

SHIDDUCH FORM

THE FOLLOWING IS A SAMPLE of a standard shidduch form based on nine forms that I obtained from various sources. These forms, which are used as general intake questionnaires, form the basis for many attempted matches. Readers will note, as discussed in the text, that many of the questions have nothing to do with determining personality, temperament or emotional levels. Rather, beyond the important basic demographic questions and one question that allows respondents to describe themselves in three to five words, many of the items are superficial and irrelevant to determining who would make a good match for whom.

PERSONAL INFORMATION

NAME: _____

ADDRESS: _____

TELEPHONE: (HOME)_____(WORK)_____(FAX)_____

E-MAIL:_____

☐ Male   ☐ Female

Date of Birth:

Height: _____ ft _____ in

MARITAL INFORMATION

Marital Status:

☐ Never married   ☐ Widowed

☐ Divorced   ☐ Other (Please explain)

If divorced, please list the rabbi who facilitated the get and the bet din that issued the get:

Do you have children?

☐ Yes (If yes, how many? Please list their ages.)

☐ No

Do the children live with you?

☐ Yes

☐ No (Please provide explanations as necessary.)

For women only: Are you eligible to marry a kohen?

EDUCATION AND OCCUPATION

What is the highest level of secular education you have achieved?
- ☐ Completed high school
- ☐ Attended college
- ☐ Graduated college
- ☐ Graduate school
- ☐ Other degree (Please explain)

Undergraduate degree major:
Graduate degree:
Current occupation:

JUDAIC BACKGROUND

What is your Judaic educational background?
(Please list names of schools attended)

Elementary school:
- ☐ Day school
- ☐ Yeshiva
- ☐ Hebrew school
- ☐ Sunday school

High school:
- ☐ Day school
- ☐ Yeshiva
- ☐ Hebrew school
- ☐ Sunday school

Did you attend yeshiva/seminary after high school?
- ☐ Yes
- ☐ No (If no, please explain)

If yes, please provide the name of the yeshiva/seminary that you attended:

Please list the shiurim, courses or chavrusas you regularly attended and their locations:

Are you:
- ☐ Observant from birth
- ☐ A baal teshuva
- ☐ A convert

If you are a baal teshuva, how long ago did you begin the process? Has your family become observant?

If you are a convert, please list the date of your conversion, the name of the bet din and the name and phone number of the presiding rabbi.

Are you:
- ☐ Ashkenazi
- ☐ Sefardi
- ☐ Mizrachi
- ☐ Other (Please specify)

Do you consider yourself:
- ☐ Chassidic
- ☐ Modern Orthodox
- ☐ Yeshivish
- ☐ Other (Please specify)

Please describe your current level of observance and religious commitment:

Are you shomer Shabbat?	☐ Yes	☐ No
Do you keep kosher?	☐ Yes	☐ No
Are you comfortable with your level of observance?	☐ Yes	☐ No

(Please explain)

Do you own a TV? ☐ Yes ☐ No
Do you watch TV regularly? (Please explain): ☐ Yes ☐ No
Do you go to movies? (Please explain): ☐ Yes ☐ No
Do you go mixed swimming? (Please explain): ☐ Yes ☐ No

Women only: Do you wear trousers?
  ☐ Yes
  ☐ No
  ☐ Sometimes (Please explain)

Women only: Do you plan to cover your hair when you are married?
  ☐ Yes
  ☐ No
  ☐ Sometimes (Please explain)

Men only: Are you a:
  ☐ Kohen
  ☐ Levi
  ☐ Yisroel

Men only: Are you comfortable with the idea of your wife wearing trousers? (Please explain)

Men only: When you are married, what are your plans for learning Torah?

Current synagogue affiliation:
Name and telephone number of rabbi:

PERSONAL CHARACTERISTICS AND INTERESTS

What do you enjoy doing in your spare time?
- ☐ Learning
- ☐ Sports
- ☐ Cultural events
- ☐ Arts and crafts
- ☐ Volunteering
- ☐ TV/movies
- ☐ Other (Please specify)

Please write three to five words that describe you:
1.
2.
3.
4.
5.

Are you willing to travel to meet someone?
- ☐ Yes (If yes, how far would you be willing to travel?)
- ☐ No

Would you be willing to relocate when you marry?　　　☐ Yes ☐ No

Are you seriously considering aliyah?　　　☐ Yes ☐ No

TELL US ABOUT THE PERSON YOU WOULD LIKE TO MEET

Age range of the person you would like to meet:

Please list three to five words that describe the person you would like to meet:

1.
2.
3.
4.
5.

Physical attributes:

Educational background:

Jewish educational background:

Would you date someone who has been married before?   □ Yes   □ No
Would you date someone who has children?   □ Yes   □ No

Does it matter if the person is:
- □   Observant from birth
- □   A baal teshuvah
- □   A convert

How about affiliation:
- □   Chasidic
- □   Modern Orthodox
- □   Yeshivish
- □   Other

Women only: Is it important that your husband:

Wear a hat?	☐ Yes	☐ No
Learn Torah regularly?	☐ Yes	☐ No
Appreciate your own Torah learning?	☐ Yes	☐ No

Men only: Is it important that your wife cover her hair?

☐ Yes (If yes, in what way?)

☐ No

REFERENCES

Please provide at least two references of people who know you well. At least one should be a rabbi.

APPENDIX II

LIST OF QUESTIONS

I HAVE COMPILED A LIST of questions asked of people who are "in the parsha" – in other words, in the process of dating. All of these questions have been verified. None were created simply for the sake of humor or are based on hearsay. All have at least two distinct verifiable sources, since they were asked by shadchanim or people seeking to arrange dates for their friends. These questions are in addition to those referred to in the text.

Although many of the questions are well-intentioned, they are highly misdirected. Some repeat the questions posted in the standard shidduch forms while others are used as follow ups. I am sure that you have heard of many of them; perhaps you were even asked some of them. While I have attempted to ascertain the motivation for some of the questions and also the best possible answers, this has not always been possible.

It is no coincidence that there are no questions regarding *middot*. Perhaps it is understood that all potential candidates for a date have impeccable manners. Nevertheless, the questions themselves say something about the *middot* of those who need this type of information. It is clear that the questions are superficial and tend to turn many people off. Nevertheless, I am sure that many who read these questions will think they are useful, even commendable, and will use them as a sort of cheat-sheet for finding the best date.

What color is the Shabbos tablecloth?

The best answer is white, though we are not sure why. Perhaps white is a symbol of the purity of Shabbos. However, there are many instances where an off-white, ivory or even light blue or green tablecloth did not impede the shidduch.

Do you stack plates on Shabbos?

We have searched for the best answer to this question and have not been able to verify the correct response. One source indicated that stacking implies that you do not use your finest china. If you used it, you would handle each plate individually. Another source told us that the only place where one may stack is at summer camp, not in one's home. Still others said that stacking moves the meal along at a more rapid pace, allowing more time for conversation and learning.

What does your mother serve at the Friday night meal?

Acceptable answers for those who request this information include chicken in any form except chicken chow mein, and perhaps roast beef. Chopped meat in any form is considered plebian. A sub-question is: Does your mother serve gefilte fish or salmon on Friday night? Since salmon is considered a more upscale dish, it is a better response despite the tradition of serving gefilte fish.

What does your mother wear to the table on Friday night?

The most acceptable response appears to be a dress or a Shabbos robe. Sub-questions are: Does your mother wear sweaters and skirts or dresses to the table?

Does the young woman wear sweaters and skirts or dresses on Shabbos?

With this question we enter the category of acceptable attire for women. The best answer remains dresses. However, I invite the reader to follow the progression of questions:

Is the potential date the kind of girl who wears denim skirts?

Depending on the time of day, the day of the week or the activity in question, the answer may be yes or no.

Do her skirts have slits?

According to those who are more rigid, the answer deemed most acceptable is "Absolutely not." However, I have been informed that it is nearly impossible to wear certain skirts without slits and be expected to walk normally. This is why so many young women and girls wear oversized skirts that tend to sweep the ground as they walk.

Do you care if she covers her toes?

This question goes well beyond the issue of hair covering. In some Chassidic environments, showing toes is not allowed. This has spilled over to other elements of the frum community. A sub-question is: Does her mother cover her toes?

In addition to the questions about the dress size of the young woman, her mother and grandmother, at least one shadchan has asked for the girl's bra size.

What does your mother wear to bed?

Lingerie is not an acceptable response to those who ask this type of question. Full-length robes or flannel nightgowns are the most acceptable responses.

What does your mother wear to take out the garbage?

"A robe" is not a good response to this question. The best answers are "She is fully dressed" or that someone else takes out the garbage, indicating that the mother has help at home from her husband, her children or a maid.

Does anyone in the family wear tee-shirts?

The wearing of tee-shirts in public is considered unacceptable for both women and men – for some, even at camp, in the summer, with long or three–quarter-length sleeves.

Financial questions tend to be more direct, if not brazen. The typical question – "Is the [woman's] father willing to support the young man?" – is a perfect example. Some financial questions are more subtle, such as:

Does the family go away for Passover?

When I was asked this question on several occasions when my name was given as a reference, the questioners told me that the family wanted to know because it was easier for their daughter to go away for the holiday than to have to make Pesach for her family. The financial implications are obvious as well.

Is the garbage pail in or out?

The garbage pail in the kitchen, that is. It seems that it is considered more correct for the kitchen garbage pail to be hidden in a cabinet, regardless of how elegant the pail may be. It is also considered a sign of greater wealth if the pail is built into a cabinet.

What kind of mother-in-law would your mother make?

This question is interesting on quite a few levels because it attempts to predict the future and address several variables simultaneously. It may refer to how willing the potential mother-in-law might be to help with cooking or child care. It may be a question of finances – will she buy expensive things for her married children? Will she meddle in the couple's affairs? This question may also address how open-minded she is – will she accept a daughter- or son-in-law who differs somewhat from her expectations? It is clear that there is no single, all-encompassing right answer. The best response I have heard to this question is "A very nice one."

How does your father address your mother?

The three individuals who were asked these questions and told me about them unanimously agreed that any affectionate nickname is considered unacceptable. These would include pet names such as "babe" or "love." "Honey" or "sweetheart" are somewhat acceptable but "Ima," "Mother" or the wife's first name are better still. One person told me that referring to her in the third person – for example, "Mrs. Rosenberg" – is considered the best protocol.

The following two questions were asked of mothers and sisters:

Is he good at math? Does he go to bed with a sefer?

In the words of one of those questioned: "Is he good at math? – Like, when he gets up to those technical gemaras, does he try to work them out or does he just skip over them?" These questions are designed to determine how much of a learner the young man is.

Then there are the questions about the father:

Where did he learn, and where does he learn now? Do his trousers fit him well? Are they too baggy or too tight, too long or too short? What color are they?

In other words, how does he present himself? Is he well-dressed and groomed or does he have little interest in his appearance? Some women prefer to date men who wear only black trousers.

Several women told me they were asked the following questions in rapid succession by different shadchanim:

> How many boys have you dated?
>
> What was the longest amount of time that you dated someone?
>
> Do you have any feelings for anyone?
>
> Have you ever been in love?
>
> What is the higher priority for you – family or job?
>
> What do you think of kollel?

All the women who were asked these questions told me they had felt like they were being interrogated as suspects in some heinous crime. The difficulty in answering these questions lies in what is considered a reasonable or fair answer. Regarding the question of how many boys a woman has dated: if the number she gives is too high, she will be seen as too picky, yet if it is too low she will be seen as naïve. Similarly, if she dated someone for a long time she may be seen as too needy, while if she dated him for a short time she will be seen once more as too picky. What is considered too long or too short a time? No one seems to know.

If a woman answers that she has feelings for someone, it means that she is still in love with a man she once dated and is not ready to move on. If she answers that she does not, this means that she is cold, distant and hard to please. Some of the women who told me about these questions also told me that they answered that they have feelings for many people. To the next question, whether they have ever been in love, they answered that they loved their family members. These were not the responses that the questioner wanted to hear.

One woman pointed out that the last two questions in these categories, priorities and kollel, are contradictory in a sense. If a woman says that she supports the idea of kollel, then her job should be the priority so that she can support the family. However, if she ranks her family over her job and the man would like his wife to have a career or profession, she has given the wrong answer. Here is the biggest problem – how can one know the answer that will satisfy the questioner's particular whim? After all, these questions and those we have discussed throughout this book have little or nothing to do with whether two particular people are right for each other.

Some questions asked of both men and women require creative, prophetic even hypothetical responses. Some examples:

What level of Kashrut do you observe?

Where do you see yourself spiritually in five years?

What seminary would you choose to attend now? (The implication is that the seminary that the prospective bride attended is not considered adequate, but perhaps if she names a more acceptable one at this point it shows that she has changed.)

Where do you see yourself living?

Are you the romantic type?

Are you the type that always remembers birthdays and gives presents?

GLOSSARY

Agunah (lit. "chained" or "anchored woman") – a "grass widow"; traditionally, a woman whose husband no longer lives with her but who cannot grant her a *get* (Jewish writ of divorce, without which she cannot remarry) because he is incapacitated or missing. In modern times, the term *agunah* (together with a more recent term, *mesorevet get*) usually refers to a woman whose husband is capable of granting her a *get* but refuses to do so, often out of spite or in order to extort money, property, custody rights or other concessions

Apikorus – Nonbeliever

Apikorsus – Heretical acts or beliefs

Bashert – Intended. In marriage, finding one's bashert is finding one's intended mate

Bet ha-midrash (lit. "house of study") – A place for the study of Torah and Talmud, usually part of a yeshiva or synagogue

Bet din (alt. bais din; pl. batei din) – Jewish court of law

Chasidic (alt. Hasidic) – lit. "pious ones." Usually refers to followers of the Chasidic movement originated by the Baal Shem Tov in Ukraine during the eighteenth century

Chazal – Jewish sages

Chessed – kindness, a kind act

Chofetz Chaim – Rabbi Israel Meir ha-Cohen Kagan (1838–1933), noted for the more than twenty works he wrote on proper speech, especially *Guarding One's Tongue* and his principal work, *Chafetz Chaim*

Choson – Bridegroom

Daven – Yiddish: to pray

Em ha-bayit – house mother

Eshet Chayil (lit. "woman of valor") – Proverbs 31:10–31, traditionally sung at the Friday evening Shabbat meal

Frum – Religiously observant, with an Orthodox implication

Gemara – the Talmud

Gemach – an abbreviation for "gemilut chesed." An organization that provides interest-free loans or lends other items

Halacha – Jewish religious law

Halachic – custom, practice or legal ruling ratified by authoritative rabbis

Harav – "great rabbi"

Haredi (alt. Charedi) – lit., "one who trembles" or "anxious one"; a member of the ultra-Orthodox community

Hashem – lit. "the Name." Refers to God.

Hashkafa (pl. hashkafot) – Jewish philosophy or one's personal worldview

Hasidic – see Chasidic

Hesder – A yeshiva program in Israel that combines advanced religious studies with military service

Kashrut (Kashrus) – the Jewish dietary laws

Kippah seruga – Knitted skullcap worn most often by modern Orthodox men

Kollel – A postgraduate institute of advanced Jewish learning for married men who receive a stipend for their study

Lashon ha-ra – lit., "evil language." Jewish concept of forbidden speech – for example, slander or defamation

Machmir – stringent; one who advocates or observes additional stringencies beyond normative practice

Middot (alt. "middos") – manners, social skills

Mekarev – to bring close (usually refers to teaching non-observant Jews about traditional Jewish observance)

Mitzvah (pl. "mitzvot") – action performed in obedience to a religious commandment; good deed

Morah – woman teacher

Motzi shem ra – to slander or libel; considered a major transgression

Parasha – the weekly Torah portion

Pasken – to render a religious ruling

Passt nisht – Yiddish for "It just isn't right," "it simply isn't done"

Posek – A rabbi who is an authority on Jewish law and renders religious rulings

Kashrut – state of being kosher, ritually fit or proper

Rambam – Rabbi Moshe ben Maimon, also known as Maimonides (1135–1204). A scholar, philosopher and physician noted for his religious and philosophical writings

Rashi – Rabbi Shlomo Yitzchaki (1040–1105). A medieval-era French sage noted for his extensive commentaries on the Torah and the Talmud

Rav – rabbi. E.g.: "He is my rav" (see Harav)

Richuk kerovim – pushing away those who are close

Rosh Yeshiva (pl. "roshei yeshiva") – senior rabbi in a yeshiva

Rebbe – The leader of a Chasidic movement

Sefer – book, usually a religious text

Shabbos (alt. "Shabbat") – Seventh day of the week, according to Jewish law the day of rest

Shadchan (pl. "shadchanim") – matchmaker

Shemirat ha-lashon (lit. guarding one's tongue) – A book written by the Chafetz Chaim on the proper use of language and ways to communicate

Shidduch – an arranged marriage

Shiur – lecture, usually on a topic of religious law or scripture

Shomer negiah – one who observes the prohibition against touching members of the opposite sex

Shul – Yiddish for "synagogue"

Shulchan Aruch (lit. "The Prepared Table") – The most complete and authoritative compilation of Jewish law since the Talmud, written by Rabbi Yosef Karo (1488–1575) in the mid-sixteenth century

Torah – The range of Jewish law and tradition, but may also refer to the Five Books of Moses

Tosafos – Explanatory writings on the Talmud by a group of medieval scholars

Treif (lit. "torn") – not kosher

Tznius – modesty; the laws of modest dress and behavior

Yeshiva – Rabbinical seminary or academy of higher Jewish learning

Yeshivish – pertaining to or part of the yeshiva world

Yichud – seclusion with a member of the opposite sex

Yichud room – a room in which the bride and groom spend several minutes alone together immediately after the wedding ceremony

Yom Tov – Jewish holiday

Michael J. Salamon, Ph.D., FPPR, has worked with the Jewish communities of the Greater New York area for more than two decades. He has been at the forefront of influencing the community to acknowledge and deal with the fact the Jewish community is confronted with the challenges that face the general community including dating and relationship issues, substance and alcohol abuse, eating and other disorders relating to body image issues, and physical abuse. He is a sought after speaker by synagogues, yeshivas, and Jewish communal institutions throughout the country. He is the author of many assessment tools including the Life Satisfaction Scale and the Addiction Dependency Scale, as well as the book *Home or Nursing Home: Making the Right Choice.* He has presented more than one hundred papers at national and international conferences.

Dr. Salamon is the founder and director of the Adult Developmental Center, Inc., a comprehensive psychological consulting practice in Hewlett, NY. He empowers individuals and families to cope with the various psychological challenges that arise throughout the life span. Among his areas of specialization are substance abuse and alcoholism counseling, crisis management, child, family, and marital counseling, therapeutic interventions, and gerontology.

Dr. Salamon received his doctorate in psychology from Hofstra University. He is a Fellow of the American Psychological Association, a Fellow of the Gerontological Society of America's Behavioral and Social Sciences Section and a board certified Diplomate-Fellow Prescribing Psychologist Register.